How to Speak

the Written Word

How to Speak the Written Word

A Guide to Effective Public Reading

by

NEDRA NEWKIRK LAMAR

REVISED AND ENLARGED

—————•◆•—————

FLEMING H. REVELL COMPANY

OLD TAPPAN, NEW JERSEY

For their patient prodding and for their capable assistance in the handling of the manuscript and in other important ways I wish to thank Miss Edwina Austin, Mrs. Harry J. Birtley, and Mrs. William Miller. And, of course, Henry Lamar.

Quotations from Webster's New International Dictionary, second edition, copyrighted 1934, 1939, 1945 by G. & C. Merriam Company, are used by permission of the publishers.

TO

KATHRYN and GEORGE NEWKIRK

and

MILO WALKER

CONTENTS

How to Speak

the Written Word

I

MATTERS OF FIRST IMPORTANCE

THE WHOLE PURPOSE of this book is to help you to read naturally. Many " trained " readers have had all the naturalness trained out of them.

The material used has been tested over a period of fifteen years by the men and women in my classes and has been found satisfyingly practical. I have tried earnestly to avoid fruitless generalities. Only the branches of the subject which can be treated more or less concretely have been discussed. For example, breathing and voice training have been scarcely mentioned, since they require personal instruction from a teacher on the spot. A book cannot find out whether you breathe in your chest or in your diaphragm and tell you what to do about it. A printed page cannot hear whether your voice is nasal, flat, or husky and tell you whether you are practicing your voice exercises correctly or incorrectly. Therefore, this book has not attempted to do so.

The principles advanced are not mere theories. That they are sound and practical and enduring has been proved by scores of students, many of whom are business men of the type frequently referred to as " hard-headed." Most have been skeptical at the outset but have convinced themselves of the common sense underlying these instructions. " ' Gentlemen, I shall not ask you to believe but defy you to deny,' said Professor Seeley when addressing a new class."—Jacques Barzun: *Teacher in America.**

A rewarding comment that those who have studied these principles frequently receive is something like this: " I've read that poem

* Quoted by permission of Little, Brown and Company and the Atlantic Monthly Press, publishers. Boston.

[or Bible verse, or hymn] many times but have never seen in it the clear meaning that you brought out. Part of it I never even understood before."

Still another characteristic of the readers who have studied and followed these instructions is that they do not speak or read alike. Their reading is not uniform or stereotyped. No one has ever told me, "I could tell right away that he was your pupil, because he reads just as you read" or "because he uses your 'method.'" The following pages set forth suggestions about how to read the various constructions of grammar, of logic, and of punctuation which the reader will find in any book. A few of these constructions must be read in a certain way and in no other way, but most of them allow some or much choice. This provides the sight-reader with a solid framework of technique but allows him the same scope for individual expression as does any other art. In many of the exercises, a method of reading a construction frequently heard will be explained as demonstrably wrong but several ways of reading it properly (that is, logically and meaningfully) will be explained. The student may take his choice of these or may think of a method of his own. Thus there is almost unlimited scope for individuality within the bounds of these principles.

Four great pianists will play the same concerto so distinctively that a musician can tell one from the other; yet each pianist will be following the principles of the science of music, principles as firm as those of mathematics. Four deft cooks will follow the same recipe for a cake and yet turn out different but delicious cakes. And yet the directions given in a cook book frequently are rigid, while the ideas set forth in this book are not. So don't be afraid that you will be copying someone else or reading like every other student of this book if you apply these instructions.

The more skeptically you approach this book, the better you will apply it—once you are convinced that its suggestions are sound. If you think it is asking you to do anything in the way of pronouncing, phrasing, or emphasizing that makes you sound peculiar, please stop and reread the instructions. Perhaps you have misread them or misunderstood them. The whole object of the book is to keep you from sounding peculiar, affected, or unnatural.

The most frequent comment about the readers and speakers who have followed these instructions is something like this: "You sound entirely natural. I have seldom heard anyone read with greater simplicity and unaffectedness." One man who, after much intensive study, developed into an outstanding reader over the radio and before groups, was told, much to his amusement, "You are an ideal reader; and I'm so glad you never did let the speech teachers get hold of you!"

Some may say that this book is too technical, even though the technical explanations have been made as simple as possible. Since oral reading is a science and an art requiring a technique, how can any honest and adequate book on the subject fail to be technical? You might as well object to a text on grammar because it is too technical.

As in any other art, however, your technique must be concealed. The listener must be unaware that there are technique and hard work behind reading or any other artistic performance. As soon as the hearer notices technical devices or receives the impression that what is being done is difficult, you should realize either that you are using the wrong technique or that you should perfect your performance. If you ever receive such a "compliment" as this: "My dear, you were wonderful! And I could easily tell that it was a very hard piece," you should devote much practice to your assignment before attempting it again. The best compliment anyone can give you runs something like this: "It sounded so easy! I just felt as if I could have done it as well myself!"

The ability to read intelligently and intelligibly is both a science and an art. Good oral readers are always applying certain principles, whether consciously or unconsciously. Usually they do so knowingly, as people seldom just happen upon either an art or a science. Almost anyone will admit that this is true of pipe organists or architects, for example, and yet many persons cannot see that it is true of oral readers, too. Possibly because there are so many poor readers and speakers, people believe that the occasional effective reader is just a person with a special gift.

Unless a violinist is one of the rare and phenomenally gifted geniuses, he must have learned his notes, he must have perfected his technique, and then he must have applied his knowledge and skill to a certain sonata before being able to play it well.

1. In the same way, a reader, to be successful and pleasing, should first of all have a thorough understanding of the selection he is to read. If he loves it and enjoys it, this is still better. But, above all, he must understand it. Surely no one will deny that this is the first *2.* essential. But the second requirement is equally important: the knowledge of how to express the meaning that he may see ever so clearly. And that involves a knowledge of where to pause and where not to pause, what to emphasize and what to subdue, and other points which will be discussed in this book.

The long-suffering listeners, either over the radio or in audiences, are so accustomed to hearing mechanical, meaningless reading that they revise mentally while they listen. But this should not be the case. The reader's function, the newsbroadcaster's function, is to give the sense, not to make his listeners have to dig it out for themselves. In the rare instances where the reader does the necessary reasoning and the consequent phrasing and emphasizing, his listeners are appreciative (" numb with surprise and gratitude," * as Wolcott Gibbs might say) and recognize him as a good reader, although they can seldom point out what the reader did in order to produce the meaningful, easy-to-follow effect.

As an oral reader you should not be like the chorus in Shakespeare's *King Henry V,* which apologizes for the inability of the small theater to represent the vast battlefields of France, requesting the audience to " piece out our imperfections with your thoughts " and " eke out our performance with your mind."

If Mr. X or Mr. Y applies the principles explained in this book, the personal peculiarities or personal interpretations will be removed from the reading and the listeners will have a chance to hear the meaning of the Biblical passage or the news broadcast instead of hearing Mr. X or Mr. Y.

You might read very familiar material, such as Biblical passages or the Gettysburg Address, in a complete chant or with all the wrong words deliberately emphasized and your readers might still be able to make out the meaning, because of their familiarity with it.

* Quoted by permission of *The New Yorker.*

But such reading would give them no pleasure and certainly would add nothing to their knowledge and appreciation of the passage.

If someone reads a passage in a perfunctory way and then some-one else reads it in a really meaningful way, the average listener probably will not, perhaps should not, realize just what the latter reader has done to produce the satisfactory effect. But he will notice the difference, just as he would notice the difference, without being able to explain it, if he heard a merely competent violinist play a selection and then heard a really great one play the same thing.

You hear it said, " He is a good reader, because he has practiced reading aloud for years " or "I'm sure she reads that poem right, because she has drilled and drilled herself on it." One might as well say, " I'm sure he has a perfect breast stroke, because he has paddled around in the water by himself every morning this summer." The amount or intensity of practice, drill, and experience has little to do with the excellence of a reader. What matters is the kind of practice. Constant drilling in the wrong way makes a reader poorer instead of better. That is why self-instruction can be so dangerous. If there is any field in which it is desirable to adopt Davy Crockett's motto, " Be sure you're right, then go ahead," it is in the field of oral read-ing.

If you master the principles and familiarize yourself with the exercises in the following pages, you will seldom run across a con-struction in your reading that you won't know how to read intelli-gently. And you yourself will see meanings that you have never noticed before and will be able to bring them out for your listeners.

Maybe you feel that you lack sufficient education to be or to become a good oral reader. Don't let this thought discourage you. Frequently a person of comparatively little formal education is or becomes a more pleasing reader than someone with much education or even with much training in subjects related to oral reading. Many times a " trained " reader has been trained in stilted, ornate methods, and often a highly educated person is less teachable than one who realizes his lack. Good, plain, honest mistakes are easier to listen to and to forgive than artificial, mannered reading.

The greatest fault and the most prevalent among oral readers is unnaturalness, in the form of stilted, dramatic, oratorical, or old-

fashioned elocutionary affectations. It is these things more than anything else that this book attempts to counteract or, better, to prevent.

I have tried to present every slightest detail that might help someone. Especially in the Answer Book the most minute points have
been explained, to an almost insulting degree. Every effort has been
made to avoid vagueness and generalities.

An outstanding feature of this book, aside from the ideas and
principles it sets forth, many of which I am convinced are original
and are to be found nowhere else, is the Answer Book. Many text-
books on mathematics and similar subjects have answer books, but I
have never run across one in a book of this nature.

If you are a serious student of the subject you will naturally not
use the Answer Book until you have tried conscientiously to work
out the exercises without it. And please don't attempt the exercises
until you have studied carefully the chapter which precedes each set
of exercises. Skimming this book will not make you a good reader
any more than skimming the telephone directory would do so. Just
reading it will not be fair either to you or to the book.

And please remember that the Answer Book is not like the answer
book in the back of an algebra text. To most of the exercises in this
book there are no cut-and-dried, right-or-wrong answers. The
" answers " offered here are merely suggested as conclusions you are
likely to reach if you accept the premises and follow the principles
set forth in the following chapters.

Part of the material in this book sets forth logical principles,
all of which can be proved by reasoning. The rest presents conversational patterns, which can be tested by listening carefully
to the way people talk. Try to avoid using the word *rule*. I feel
that there isn't a rule in this book; that is, there is no dictum that
I have just made up.

It is the logical principles that show you the meaning, while
the conversational patterns show you how to read out the meaning in a natural way, as if you were just talking.

Probably the principle that shows the most meaning, or that
reveals it most often, is the one regarding the relative emphasis
of nouns and adjectives. If you are really alert to this principle,

you will keep discovering more meaning in what you read. A thorough understanding of the behavior of restrictives and non-restrictives and of two things grammatically connected with a third is extremely important, as is conversance with the principle dealing with what something modifies or belongs with. And the content of the whole first chapter on emphasis is of primary importance.

If, after reading the whole book, you continue to go over these headings until they become a part of the way you look at a page, you will find the meaning comes popping out at you.

Of the conversational patterns, the most significant are the consideration of connecting words followed by parenthetical expressions, and the handling of pronoun objects of prepositions. But they merely help you to give out the meaning in the manner in which you talk, and are not so vital as the principles that show you the meaning *to* give out.

One more important caution: Do not read this book in one gulp. The material it contains, especially in the exercises and the Answer Book, is highly concentrated and intensely detailed. Take it in small doses.

You will notice that most of the examples and exercises are verses from the Bible. They have been chosen instead of other literary passages, not because this book is concerned primarily with Bible-reading but because it is concerned primarily with any form of oral reading and because the Bible is not only the most rewarding but also probably the most difficult material to read aloud satisfactorily. If you can read the Bible aloud well, you can read anything— even the poems of Robert Browning. If you can read the Old Testament intelligently at sight you can read a news flash sensibly or you can give a successful sight reading in a theatrical manager's office.

It was with the hope that it would be of practical help to the teacher and students in the classroom as well as to the student far removed from teachers and classes that this book was written. And if it helps a radio announcer or an oral reader, it will help his listeners as well.

II

WHAT TO EMPHASIZE

New and Old Ideas

The whole purpose of this chapter is to help you to emphasize naturally, as in conversation.

Meaningful emphasis and natural phrasing are the two qualities employed by radio speakers who read from a prepared script but sound as if they are ad libbing or speaking the words just as they come to thought. Either consciously or unconsciously they employ certain principles of emphasis and phrasing; probably they do so consciously. Some radio announcers, on the other hand, obviously are reading printed words, emphasizing the wrong words, and pausing where they would never pause in conversation. If any reader will master the principles set forth in this book he will be able to read as if he were just talking. And his sight reading will improve unbelievably.

This book has been compiled to help all readers, especially two very numerous groups: radio announcers or commentators and Bible readers. It might seem that reading news broadcasts and reading the Bible have little in common, but, whether he is reading the report of the latest strike or one of the most inspiring passages in the Bible, the reader is merely trying to give the sense to the listener and he is trying to read as though he were not reading but just talking naturally.

Attempting to dictate to people how to read the Bible would be presumptuous and almost sacrilegious. At no place in this book will the reader be told what a scriptural passage " means." Therefore, the students of these instructions will not be enticed into that rightfully dreaded thing called " interpretation."

Simple Contrast. The whole secret of meaningful, and therefore natural, emphasis lies in stressing the word that carries the thought, the meaning-word. To put it more fully:

EMPHASIZE THE NEW IDEA OR THE CONTRAST; SUBDUE THE OLD IDEA. It is odd that many professional actors and speakers apparently have never discovered this obviously sound principle nor been told it by their teachers and coaches. Yet Lewis Carroll, not a speaker but a mathematician and a writer, realized it and expressed it clearly in the quotation given in Florence Becker Lennon's biography of him: " My rule for knowing which word to lean on is the word that tells you something new, something that is different from what you expected."—*Victoria Through the Looking-Glass* (Published by Simon and Schuster, Inc., New York).

Suppose you said to a newly-arrived visitor: " This is a very comfortable chair. Won't you sit in this chair? " Probably you would slightly stress *comfortable* and *chair* in the first sentence. Would you stress *chair* in the second sentence? Certainly not. Try it that way and see how absurd it sounds. You have already introduced the subject of the chair and stressed it. It was a new and important idea, the meaning-word, in the first sentence. In the second sentence it is an old idea, something now taken for granted and not worth stressing. But the thing you're now interested in is not the chair but the sitting in it. *Sit* is the new idea and so you emphasize it. " This is a very **comfortable chair**. Won't you **sit** in this chair? "

The second *chair* is such an old, taken-for-granted idea, in fact, that you would be even more likely to leave it out altogether and substitute the little pronoun *it*. " This is a very comfortable chair. Won't you sit in it? "

Now, remember that a pronoun is a word with no meaning of its own. By derivation and by definition it is merely a word used for a noun. When the meaning of the noun is so obvious that you don't even bother to express it but use instead a mere substitute word, you hardly need to stress the substitute.

(This does not mean that pronouns are never to be stressed, however. Sometimes you emphasize them to express contrast, as: " This is not **his** but **hers**." " I chose **you**, not **her**.")

Read these sentences aloud: " Florence is my sister. I love

Florence." Probably you stressed the first *Florence* and *sister*. But surely you didn't stress the second *Florence,* because it is now an old idea. Instead, if you read it naturally, you subdued the second *Florence* and stressed *love,* which is the new idea. The second *Florence* is so obvious that the more natural thing to say would be " Florence is my sister. I love her."

Frequently the " new idea " is more than just a new idea: it is a definite contrast. "Honesty is the best policy: dishonesty, therefore, should be avoided." Here *dishonesty* would naturally receive the greatest stress of any word in the sentence, because it is not only a new idea but a pointed contrast to *honesty.*

This stressing of the contrast is so natural and automatic in spontaneous speaking that we stress not only the word but the particular syllable of that word that brings out the contrast. The dictionary pronunciation of *dishonesty* accents the second syllable, as we all do normally. But to accent it that way in this sentence would be to rob it of sense. Try it aloud that way. No, the syllable *dis-* is what brings out the contrast between *honesty* and *dishonesty;* so, in spontaneously speaking these words, we would accent it on the first syllable, since in conversation we are not thinking of dictionaries, spellers, and grammars; we are thinking of the sense.

This principle is used unconsciously and almost unfailingly in unrehearsed speech. Even in the well-known Latin conjugation of *amare* whoever heard anyone accent the words as they should be accented: am*o*—am*as*—am*at?* Not only high-school freshmen but even many teachers of Latin never think of accenting it any other way than am*o*—am*as*—am*at,* so strongly impelled are we to emphasize the new idea or the contrast and subdue the old idea.

Double Contrast; Multiple Contrast. Sometimes we find sentences containing a double contrast: not just one thing contrasted with another but also a third thing contrasted with a fourth. " The course you recommend leads to progress but the policy he sanctions leads to disaster." In this sentence only four words need emphasis; to emphasize more would be to clutter the sentence and cloud the meaning. They are the four words that bring out a double contrast: *You* contrasted with (or balanced by) *he* and *progress* contrasted with (or balanced by) *disaster*. You could almost suggest the meaning of the sentence with these four words alone: "You—progress; he—disaster."

Now let's see why we do not emphasize the other words in the sentence. There are very good reasons for subduing some of the others. There is no special reason for subduing *course* and *recommend*, except that their importance is greatly overshadowed by *you* and *progress* and you mustn't emphasize so many words that you lose all emphasis. But there is a very specific reason for subduing *policy*: it is an old idea. But, you may say, the word *policy* hasn't been used before. No, the word hasn't but the idea has, because *policy* in this sentence means about the same as *course*. They could be interchanged, in fact, without altering the meaning. Remember always that you are dealing with ideas, with meanings, and not merely with words. Also, the "oldness" of the idea may be merely implied. You subdue *sanctions*, too, since it is an old idea, carrying about the same meaning as *recommend*. And of course you subdue the second *leads*, since it is identical with the first *leads*. Still more, you could leave out the second *leads* altogether: "The course you recommend leads to progress; the policy he sanctions, to disaster." In fact, the sentence could have been written to omit all three words which there are definite reasons to subdue, *policy, sanctions,* and *leads*: "Your course leads to progress; his, to disaster." The sentence hasn't lost a thing except excess words. The meaning is the same. This proves the soundness of the principle just set forth, since **any word you can leave out without changing the meaning you need not and should not stress.**

Readers are more likely to emphasize too many words than too few. This mistake is almost as bad as emphasizing the wrong words. Stressing all the words in a sentence is like underscoring all the words in a letter: when you have done so you might as well not have stressed or underscored any of them. You are back on a level of no emphasis at all.

Sometimes readers deliberately try to emphasize too many or too few words, or try to keep from giving any pronounced emphasis, because they do not know these principles for digging into a sentence to extract its essential meaning. Emphasizing too many words clutters the meaning of a sentence. Decide which ones should be definitely stressed and which should be definitely subdued. Then devote as much care to subduing as to stressing.

Do not stress the first of a pair of contrasted words as heavily as the second or you will produce the effect of hitting words or plugging, which can become a mannerism annoying to your hearers. You don't have to knock your hearers down to show them you know where the emphasis belongs and you must give them credit for being able to catch the meaning without having everything heavily underscored for them.

Different Parts of Speech Contrasted. Notice that the two words contrasted are not necessarily the same parts of speech: don't expect that a noun must be contrasted with a noun, a verb with a verb, etc. It cannot be repeated too often that you are working with ideas, with thoughts, with meanings, and not with words or with parts of speech. "Fewer prisoners have been taken in Japan than in the European war." Unbelievable as it seems, a news announcer read this with the emphasis on *war*. The implied contrast is between prisoners in the war with Japan and prisoners in the war in Europe. Therefore, although *European* is an adjective and *Japan* a noun, they are contrasted and are the words to be most heavily stressed in this sentence.

"Among birds the male parent is more likely to accept responsibility than among the four-footed creatures."

Read this sentence aloud. Which words did you heavily emphasize? *Parent? Footed?* Or, still worse, *creatures?* That's the way constructions of this type often are stressed and this reading misses the point almost completely. First recast the sentence: The male parent among birds (rather) than among the four-footed creatures is more likely to accept responsibility. Or, if you object to inserting the word *rather:* The male parent among birds is more likely to accept responsibility than among the four-footed creatures.

Now you see that *birds* and *four* are the only words that receive heavy emphasis, since the whole point of the sentence is to contrast the habits of the male parent among birds with the male parent among animals, or four-footed creatures. Stressing *creatures* is utterly pointless, because it is so unimportant, both kinds of animal being creatures, that you could leave it out entirely without affecting the meaning or the clarity of the sentence. "Among the four-footed" is just as clear as "among the four-footed creatures." *Four-footed*, not *creatures*, is the meaning-word, as *four-footed* is contrasted with *birds* (the two-footed). Therefore, stressing *footed* is not so bad as stressing *creatures*, because *footed* is at least part of the meaning-word; but it is not the more meaningful part. *Four* is the word that carries the meaning, since it makes the contrast with *two* (or *two-footed*) implied in *birds*.

A slight emphasis on *male* is sensible, since, after all, there is an implied contrast with the female parent. No stress should be given to *parent*, as you could leave it out altogether without taking too much from the clarity. *Accept-responsibility* almost crystallizes into one word, with the stress on *responsibility*. Stressing *accept* would imply a contrast with *reject*, which is not the most important point of the sentence. The whole idea behind the sentence is the contrast between the behavior of the father-bird and the behavior of the father-animal, and *birds* and *four* are the words that convey this contrast. Therefore, try reading it with heavy emphasis on *birds* and *four* and light emphasis on *male* and *responsibility* and with no stress at all on *parent* and *creatures*.

"Among **birds** the **male** parent is more likely to accept **responsibility** than among the **four-footed** creatures."

Implied New or Old Idea; Implied Contrast. Now let's consider the **implied** new or old idea. In a sentence like "Honesty is the best policy; dishonesty, therefore, should be avoided," the contrast is clearly expressed in two words of definitely opposite meaning, *honesty* and *dishonesty*. It would be hard to read this sentence without stressing *dishonesty*, which brings out the contrast. But not all contrasts label themselves so plainly. In some sentences the contrasts are merely implied and the reader must learn to recognize such constructions and be on the lookout for them, or he will fail to give his readers a clear idea of the sense.

"Some trappers and fishermen were alarmed by the meteor but

few citizens knew that it had fallen." At first glance you may not see any contrast here. But analyze it carefully. Isn't it safe to suppose that trappers and fishermen are citizens? Then, by implication, the word *citizens* is an old idea, left over from *trappers* and *fishermen*. Then *few* is a new idea, almost a contrast, by implication, and should be stressed, and *citizens* is implied to be an old idea and should be thrown away. Yet this sentence was read by a news broadcaster with the stress on *citizens,* suggesting that, since *citizens* is stressed, it must be a new idea and that trappers and fishermen, therefore, are not citizens. Try reading the sentence in an expanded form and see whether you don't almost automatically stress *few* and subdue *citizens:* " Some citizens who were trappers and some citizens who were fishermen were alarmed by the meteor but few citizens knew that it had fallen."

Don't feel at this point that the subject is involved and difficult. With a little observation and practice you will be surprised to see that you can detect these implied new or old ideas as easily as the clearly expressed ones. You will become so conscious of them that they will almost pop out at you from the printed page and your reading will gain greatly in meaning, especially your sight reading. And your listeners will notice the difference but most of them won't realize what you are doing to bring out the meaning.

Synonyms Expressing New or Old Ideas. Another thing to watch for is synonyms expressing new or old ideas. Sometimes an old idea is expressed not by the same word but by a synonym, a word that means almost exactly the same thing. " On wings of fiction we fly to happier lands; or we lose ourselves just as pleasantly when borne on melody's pinions." Both *wings* and *fiction* are to be emphasized, and so is *melody's,* since it is contrasted with *fiction;* but *pinions* certainly should be slighted, since it means the same thing as *wings.* There is no repetition of words here but a repetition of ideas. Try substituting *wings* for *pinions:* " On wings of fiction we fly to happier lands; or we lose ourselves just as pleasantly when borne on melody's wings." You naturally subdue the second *wings.* So you should subdue its equivalent, *pinions.*

Carry-over; Different Meaning at Different Times. We have seen

that we sometimes use one pronunciation of a word at one time and
another at another. We normally accent *dishonesty* on the second
syllable but if we have just been talking about *honesty* we naturally
depart from the dictionary pronunciation and accent the first
syllable. We do this because the *-honesty* part of the word has
become an old idea and we want to stress *dis-*, which is the new idea.
Thus we carry over the thought from one sentence into the next.

Suppose you are reading aloud this quotation from Shakespeare:

> "Love is too young to know what conscience is:
> Yet who knows not, conscience is born of love?"

Probably you will conclude that the indispensable words in the
first line are *love, young, conscience, is,* and, perhaps, *know.* In the
second line you could get by with stressing just one word, *born,*
because the first four words are not especially important and *conscience* and *love* are decidedly unimportant, being old ideas. But
born is essential, being a new idea. Your voice will rise in pitch
steadily through *born* and then drop for the last two words. Thus,
born will be emphasized by increased volume and by higher pitch.
Some readers might like to emphasize *who* and *not;* this would not
be strictly necessary but would still be an intelligent reading. This
is a place for individual choice but there is no choice about stressing
born, if you want to bring out the sense.

But suppose that at another time you read this quotation immediately after having read these other lines from Shakespeare:

> "My conscience hath a thousand several tongues,
> And every tongue brings in a different tale,
> And every tale condemns me for a villain."

Now, if you read the other two lines you will carry over the
meaning by stressing differently. Instead of leaning heavily on *conscience* you will subdue it, since it is an old idea. You will stress *love*
and *young* as essential new ideas, and this time you will almost have
to stress either *know* or *is,* or both. This allows at least three different "correct" readings of this line. The only thing they have in

common is stressing *love* and *young* and subduing *conscience*. Doesn't this rule out the danger of uniformity and insure individuality in reading?

Failure to use this carry-over of ideas from one quotation to another or even from one sentence or phrase to another means only one thing: the reader is not thinking. He does not see the connection himself and certainly he cannot give it to his hearers. This is one of the most frequent failings of Bible readers; they read each verse as if it had no connection at all with what has gone before. They merely give out each verse or sentence as it comes along, producing a chopped effect and compelling the reader either to miss the point or to have to dig out the meaning for himself. And a reader who has no carry-over frequently reads too fast, also, leaving his hearers little time for figuring out the meaning.

Practice reading Revelation 10:10. " And I took the little book out of the angel's hand, and ate it up; and it was in my mouth sweet as honey: and as soon as I had eaten it, my belly was bitter." Probably you placed only a small amount of stress on *took* and *ate* and stressed *up* rather heavily; more than likely you emphasized *mouth, sweet, honey, belly,* and *bitter*. This reading is logical.

This time read Revelation 10:9 first. " And I went unto the angel, and said unto him, Give me the little book. And he said unto me, Take it, and eat it up; and it shall make thy belly bitter, but it shall be in thy mouth sweet as honey." Now read the tenth verse. If you read it with the same emphasis you used before, you are separating it completely from verse 9, merely feeding your listeners a disconnected verse at a time. Now try stressing each *was* and soft-pedaling *mouth, sweet, honey, belly,* and *bitter*. This gives the idea that it **was** as the angel said it would be. Some readers might like to emphasize *took* and *ate* and subdue *up* in verse 10. This suggests the obvious meaning that " I **did** take the book and I **did** eat it up."

The beautiful words of John 11:25 are often read by themselves, away from the preceding and following verses, and the readers usually and rightly emphasize *resurrection,* as well as *life*. " Martha saith unto him, I know that he shall rise again in the resurrection at the last day. Jesus saith unto her, I am the resurrection, and the

life: he that believeth in me, though he were dead, yet shall he live"
(John 11:24, 25). Because verse 25 is read so often by itself and
with this same emphasis, people generally emphasize it the same way
even when they read it immediately after the preceding verse. But in
verse 24 *resurrection* is a new idea and this makes it an old idea now
in verse 25. This time *I* is the important word to emphasize, because
it is a new idea or contrast. Try reading it this way, stressing *I* and
subduing *resurrection,* and see how it carries over the thought from
the preceding verse. You may like it even better to pause after
resurrection, letting your voice fall, and then start afresh on a new
thought, emphasizing *life.*

Most readers logically stress *not, Lord,* and *physicians* in II
Chronicles 16:12. "And Asa in the thirty and ninth year of his
reign was diseased in his feet, until his disease was exceeding great:
yet in his disease he sought not to the Lord, but to the physicians."
They subdue the second *disease,* whether or not they realize that
they are doing so because it is an old idea. Some readers like to
stress the third *in* and this also is a logical way of reading it. But, if
you read this twelfth verse immediately after reading the eighth
verse of this same chapter, see how the emphasis shifts in verse 12:
"Were not the Ethiopians and the Lubims a huge host, with very
many chariots and horsemen? Yet, because thou didst rely on the
Lord, he delivered them into thine hands." Verse 8 brings out the
fact that in battle Asa relied on the Lord. Verse 12 shows that in
his disease he did not; he relied on physicians instead. Then
shouldn't you emphasize the new thoughts, second *disease, not,* and
physicians, and subdue *Lord,* an old thought?

Here is an important warning: Don't force. Don't try to get out
or to put in meanings that may not be there. Remember that you
don't want to sound as if you had been "taking lessons" or reading
books on the subject of oral reading. To try to wring out too much
meaning, through overuse of emphasis or phrasing, is as unpleasant
a fault as to read in a meaningless monotone. In John 8:38 it would
be possible to work out a quadruple contrast; you could contrast the
first *I* with the first *ye, speak* with *do,* the second *I* with the second
ye, and *my* with *your.* (" I speak that which I have seen with my

Father: and ye do that which ye have seen with your father.") But this would surely be a labored and undesirable way to read this verse.

In the book of Job is an example of one of the longest carried-over ideas in the Bible, with probably the longest separation between the two parts. The sixth and seventh verses of Job 1 are repeated almost exactly, except for one word, in the first two verses of Job 2:

"Now there was a day when the sons of God came to present themselves before the Lord, and Satan came also among them. And the Lord said unto Satan, Whence comest thou? Then Satan answered the Lord, and said, From going to and fro in the earth, and from walking up and down in it. . . . Again there was a day when the sons of God came to present themselves before the Lord, and Satan came also among them to present himself before the Lord. And the Lord said unto Satan, From whence comest thou? And Satan answered the Lord, and said, From going to and fro in the earth, and from walking up and down in it."

Sometimes readers who do not know about the principles of new-and-old ideas practice these passages over dozens of times and then turn out a reading like this: They pause after *day,* illogically, as *when the sons of God came to present themselves before the Lord* is a restrictive modifier of *day,* not nonrestrictive. It isn't just " a day," just any day; it's " a day when the sons of God came to present themselves before the Lord." (Aren't *Satan* and *also* two of the most meaningful words in the verse? Of course it's important that the sons of God came, but Satan came, too.) Another mistake in emphasis is stressing *comest* instead of *thou,* in verse 7. It doesn't mean, Why have you **come?** It means, Why have **you** come? (The others were expected but why have **you** come?) Laborious and un-thought-out reading also puts pauses after *to* and *up* in verse 7. It isn't important that he went *to* and then went *fro,* that he walked *up* and then walked *down.* This indiscriminate pausing not only robs the reading of all rhythm and climax but focuses attention on details that are comparatively unimportant, thereby obscuring the salient ideas. *To-and-fro* are almost one word and so are *up-and-down.*

The first two verses of Job 2 are almost one hundred per cent repetition, old idea, echo, carry-over, except for the first word. To read it as such is the only effective reading, whether you have read all the intervening verses or have omitted some of them or all. Really, *again* should be stressed and all the rest of verses 1 and 2 soft-pedaled. You want to produce the effect of saying merely, " Again it happened." However, it would be very difficult to subdue two whole verses, especially if you have separated the echo verses from their antecedents by reading the intervening verses. But at least you can read through the first *Lord* and perhaps through the whole first verse without much emphasis, and you can read the second verse lower and with less emphasis than normal.

If you announce a passage from I Corinthians, read a verse or two, and then announce a passage from II Corinthians, it is certainly natural to stress *Second* and subdue *Corinthians*. (Of course, if you read such a long passage from 1 Corinthians that the echo of I Corinthians does not carry over there would be no reason to stress *Second*.)

The principles of meaningful reading are akin to the art of chiaroscuro in painting. Chiaroscuro (kyah'ro-sku'ro) is an Italian word meaning light-and-shadow. Can you imagine a picture in which everything was painted in bright light and there were no shadows at all? The picture would be meaningless. In photography a brilliant object is not placed near another equally bright. A bright figure is shown next to something dark and thus is said to " exist." Likewise, in reading aloud one should have bright or foreground words (stressed) and dark or background words (subdued).

Naturally you must see something of the sense of a sentence before you can locate new and old ideas, contrasts, etc. But, once you begin digging for such things, more and more meaning reveals itself, especially in philosophical and religious readings. Many speakers and readers who have applied these principles have commented on this fact with surprise and satisfaction. It is a circular process: the more meaning you bring out, the more you see; the more meaning you see, the more you bring out.

It is not going too far to say that this principle of contrast or new-

and-old idea is the most important thing for a reader to know. Readers who have grasped it, either by being taught it or by discovering it for themselves, say that it has done more than any other one thing to make their reading simpler and more meaningful, more natural. Why? Because it is the deliberate reproduction of the way people talk in spontaneous conversation. When once you see it, it is so obvious that you wonder why you haven't realized it before.

The best-known method of stressing is to increase the volume, to pronounce the important word louder. Another method used almost as much, either consciously or unconsciously, is to raise the pitch as well as the volume, to speak the emphatic word on a higher key of the musical scale than the rest of the sentence.

Don't ever just decide on a way to phrase and emphasize and then mechanically read the sentence that way. You are merely copying your own reading of the sentence instead of thinking of the meaning each time. You must think it each time, just as if for the first time. However, once you think you have seen the meaning and the words that should be subdued and stressed to bring out the meaning, you will naturally stress the same way each time, not merely because you have underscored some words and crossed out others but because thinking of the meaning each time would make such emphasizing inevitable. There are two exceptions to this policy. There may be several ways to emphasize a passage and still bring out the meaning; for variety you can stress differently at different times. But you must decide in advance which way you will stress or you may blunder into thoughtless emphasis. The other reason for changing your emphasis is the discovery that you haven't seen the meaning clearly or haven't been emphasizing and subduing the right words to show the real meaning. Of course, in this case you should never let pride or fear of criticism keep you from changing your emphasis.

When you wish to give importance to a whole passage rather than merely to one word, you can change your tempo by slowing your rate of speed. Suddenly to speak more slowly arrests the attention of your listeners and concentrates their thought on the passage you wish to stress. Still another, and far less obvious, way is to speak decidedly softer instead of louder, sometimes to use only a whisper.

This is good for mysterious or shivery effects, especially, but may be used to some extent for other purposes. The sudden change in volume is what arrests the listener's attention. More than one actor has found that when the audience begins to grow restless, dropping the voice to a very confidential tone or even a whisper will regain and hold attention. Perhaps this is due to a wish to hear or overhear something that is very confidential or private. At any rate, if the device is not used too often it is effective.

Degrees of Emphasis. We give very light stress to merely new ideas, heavier to distinction but not quite contrast. "He has truthfulness and integrity." You give light stress to *truthfulness,* a new idea, heavier to *integrity. Integrity* is not a contrast to *truthfulness,* but is slightly different, distinguishing honesty in general from honesty in speaking. If you say one room is pink and the other green, you give a still heavier stress to *green,* which presents not merely a distinction but a light contrast.

In John 14:25 and 26, *these,* each *I, Comforter, he,* and the first *all* carry as heavy a contrast as is possible. (See Page 177)

Raising pitch for stress does not mean using a rising inflection. It means using a high pitch on the accented syllable of the stressed word. You would raise your pitch very slightly on *truth-* (in *truthfulness*), a bit higher on *-teg-* (in *integrity*), still higher on *green,* and highest of all on *these,* each *I, Com-* (in *Comforter*), *he,* and the first *all.*

If this seems mechanical or if the effect seems strained and peculiar, don't try to force it. Try to **think** the degrees of stress and let the thought show up in your pitch.

III

OTHER ASPECTS OF EMPHASIS

FIRST-TIME-NESS

THERE IS ONE outstanding characteristic of the actor who reads lines naturally or the announcer who reads a radio script as if he were just talking. That is what has been called "first-time-ness." This means the quality of sounding as if you were saying the words for the first time, as if neither you nor anyone else had even thought them before.

Of course, this ability is difficult to capture. To memorize a line of dialogue and practice it over and over and yet make it sound each time as if the thoughts were coming to you for the first time is a little like trying to unscramble eggs. But the principles of emphasis and phrasing explained in this book, if applied faithfully and skilfully, produce a convincing effect of first-time-ness. Judicious emphasizing (which includes judicious subduing) plays the most important part in achieving first-time-ness.

One of the main things to avoid is anticipating. Because you have practiced a line or a paragraph, you know "what's coming." But you are supposed always to be saying a thing and thinking a thing for the first time. You must make your audience feel that each idea, each phrase, is coming to you just at the moment you utter it.

One way to avoid anticipating is to keep yourself from unduly stressing the first part of a contrast that you are about to make. Suppose you have practiced reading the whitewashing chapter from *Tom Sawyer*.* Look at this sentence: " You see, Aunt Polly's awful particular about this fence—right here on the street, you know—

---

* From *The Adventures of Tom Sawyer,* by Mark Twain. Copyrighted by Harper & Brothers. Used by permission.

32

but if it was the back fence I wouldn't mind and **she** wouldn't." A
very poor reader might emphasize at random or emphasize a different word each time he read it, for no reason. A reader with " a
little learning " might see that there are two important contrasts
here: between *this fence* and *the back fence* and between *I* and *she*.
So he might stress *this* and *back,* and *I* and *she*. He would thus show
that he understood what he was reading about but he would not be
a good reader, that is, a " natural " reader. He would be taking in
the main ideas but not giving them out in the most effective way.

Assume that you are Tom saying (thinking) these words for the
first time. What are you thinking about? The fence. Probably you
haven't thought far enough ahead to decide to bring the back fence
into the discussion. That's why you wouldn't stress *this*. To do so
would show that you had "read ahead" through thirteen words,
two dashes, and a comma. In fact, you wouldn't stress even the first
fence. *Fence* is already an old idea. It's what all the discussion has
been about. So you subdue both *this* and *fence*. The new idea is
particular, which you stress. Then the next thought that comes to
you is rather parenthetical: the reason for being particular about it.
Next it occurs to you to bring in the back fence, for the purpose of
further bringing out your point. *Back* is not only a new idea but a
contrast; so of course you emphasize it, subduing the second *fence,*
a very old idea. At first you intend to say simply that you wouldn't
mind their whitewashing the back fence, and *mind* is the main
thought to emphasize. Then you quickly think about Aunt Polly's
part in it: **she** wouldn't either. To stress *I* shows that you are looking too far ahead. Your contrasts are too neat and well-thought-out
for spontaneous speech. Of course, *she* would be emphasized, being
new idea and contrast, as Mark Twain shows with italics.

First-time-ness is desirable particularly in reading very familiar
passages, such as parts of the Bible and of Shakespeare. " Wherefore art thou Romeo? " has been said so often that it is now to many
persons just a quotation, a mere chunk of words whose actual meaning is almost lost in familiarity. Actors sometimes practice stressing each word in turn to see whether they can figure out some fresh
interpretation. But with many well-known passages you don't have to
descend to such a mechanical device as that in order to find an

unworn way of reading them. And often the fresh or unused way is the one really meaningful way.

Even readers who ought to know better read part of the Gettysburg Address in the time-honored, sing-song way: ". . . and that government of the people, by the people, for the people shall not perish from the earth." For years I have told my pupils that that probably was not the way Lincoln read it on the battlefield. It had not yet become a quotation; he was actually thinking it, almost ad libbing it, according to one legend. What was he thinking about? A famous slogan containing three prepositional phrases, including a triple contrast? Hardly. He was thinking of popular government, government of the **people**. He was not thinking of government of the people. So he must have stressed *people* even more than *government* and he must have given little if any emphasis to *of.* In the next thought, however, he possibly stressed the preposition *by,* because it is the only new idea in the phrase. For the same reason he may have emphasized *for.* The second and third *people* are old ideas but in this case are still important.

Try reading it this way and you may agree that the passage gains freshness, almost as if you had never heard it before. Because I had long felt sure that this was the meaningful way to read it, I was gratified to read in the *Reader's Digest* a short anecdote by Ted Hatlen, telling of an old man who had heard Lincoln at Gettysburg. He reported that everyone made the mistake of saying " of the people " but that Lincoln had said " government of the **people**."

A similar passage is found in Romans 11:36: "for of him, and through him, and to him, are all things." If it is read immediately following the thirty-fifth verse, there is some reason for stressing *of* and subduing *him,* as you could consider *of* a new idea and *him* a carried-over idea. But often it is read in such a setting that the previous reference to *him* is farther away; in this case, it gives a fresher approach to a very familiar verse if you do not stress *of* so much and do not subdue *him* so thoroughly. When there is a choice of two logical readings, it seems always better to take the fresher. And yet it is never good to use a new reading if it is labored or spectacular or if you are doing so merely to startle or impress.

"Ye cannot serve God and mammon." This sentence from Matthew 6:24 is another often-quoted passage and the last three words have come to be read almost like one word, God-and-mammon, as though it were just one thing. However, it is not only two separate things but two directly opposite things; so there should be at least a slight pause before *and* and you could even stress *and*.

But there are times when the writer seems definitely looking towards a contrast. In passages like this it is not sensible to labor for a forced first-time-ness. Suppose you are reading in a broadcast a sentence like this: "One of the tubes will be used for transmitting sound, the other for receiving." The writer almost undoubtedly was thinking of the two types at the same time and had intended at the outset to make the contrast. So it sounds peculiar to subdue *transmitting* and stress *sound*. The whole purpose of the sentence, apparently, is to contrast *transmitting* with *receiving*.

Some idiomatic expressions have become so crystallized, in English and in other languages, that the words taken separately do not have any meaning. Expressions like *from day to day* and *from everlasting to everlasting* are almost in this class. They have really become almost one word and it would be foolish to reason that you must stress each *to* as contrasts, and subdue second *day* and second *everlasting* as old ideas. The only sensible way to read them is the way they are always read, with each *day* and each *everlasting* emphasized and with the prepositions subdued.

Unless there is some unusual reason for doing otherwise, it is sensible to say simply *thick-and-thin, ups-and-downs,* etc.

Interrupted Speeches. One of the most difficult things for an actor or a reader to handle effectively is an interrupted speech: a speech broken off by someone else or by oneself.

"The Queen turned crimson with fury, and, after glancing at her for a moment like a wild beast, screamed, 'Off with her head! Off—'

"'Nonsense!' said Alice, very loudly and decidedly, and the Queen was silent."—Lewis Carroll: *Alice's Adventures in Wonderland.*

Suppose these quotafions are the lines of a play and you are playing the part of the Queen. You want to sound as if you are really interrupted on the second *off* and you want to sound as if you didn't know you were going to be interrupted. The worst way to read the line, the way in which such lines are often read, is the way that indicates clearly that you know the other actor is supposed to interrupt you and you are just waiting for him to do so. You show it by emphasizing and holding the last word, instead of saying it quickly and giving it no more emphasis than you would if you didn't expect to be interrupted.

As most actors know, the best way is to figure out what the whole speech would be if it were completed. Then actually start to say the whole thing and, when the other actor cuts you off, you will sound natural because you will actually be interrupted. The whole speech here would obviously have been " Off with her head! " And so you start to say the whole thing.

Another good reason for planning to say the whole speech is that sometimes the actor who is supposed to interrupt you forgets to come in on time. Or maybe he forgets his speech altogether. If you are left standing with an unfinished speech in your mouth it will seem to the audience that it is you who have forgotten the lines. But if you are able to finish your sentence it will be clear that it is the other actor who is at fault.

Still another advantage, less selfish than the last, is that it is easier to cover the fact that someone has forgotten a line if you can complete your own line. It makes it easier for either you or the other actor to ad lib until somebody picks up the right line.

Now suppose that you are giving a reading of the whole play yourself and you have to impersonate both the Queen and Alice. This is much more difficult, of course. You have to interrupt yourself. The only way to do it convincingly is to imagine vividly that you are going to complete the sentence. This will help you to start the " Off—" with no more emphasis than you should use and to let go of it quickly by shouting with a different type of voice, " Nonsense! "

The knack of reading *a* hesitating or stammering speech is very simple. In the following quotation do not draw out the first *I*. Listen to the way you say the second *I* in the completed sentence. (" Surely you know that I—I can never thank you.") Say the first *I* quickly and with little stress and do not hold it; imagine again that you are intending to complete the sentence but you suddenly stop. If you read it naturally, the first *I* will be said so quickly and will stop so suddenly that it will be little more than a click in your throat.

Try reading this sentence: " I can't describe it exactly but it's— it's—well, it's—like a—a sudden plunge into icy water." The amateurish way to read it would be to stress and hold on to each *it's* and each *a* and—still worse—to pronounce each *a* as long a. (The indefinite article, unless stressed, is simply *uh*.) Try to make yourself believe that you are going to say, " I can't describe it exactly but it's like a sudden plunge into icy water." Then cut yourself suddenly on the first *it's,* saying it quickly and making it staccato. Next, imagine that you are going to say, " It's like a sudden plunge into icy water." Cut off *it's* in the same way. Do the same with each *a,* making yourself believe each time that you are going to complete the sentence. This is a feat of self-deception equal to the White Queen's cultivated ability to believe as many as six impossible things before breakfast. But with practice you can, like the White Queen, get the knack of it.

Professional and literary writers are not given to frequent use of dashes. They leave the pauses up to the judgment or cleverness of the reader or actor. A pause made at an unexpected place can make the difference between mediocre and artistic line-reading. When Sydney Carton and the little seamstress in Dickens' *A Tale of Two Cities* descend from the tumbril and await their turns to be guillotined, she says, " I mind nothing while I hold your hand. I shall mind nothing when I let it go, if they are rapid." An amateurish reader might read the last sentence, or at least the last clause, with no pause. But see how it gains effectiveness, vividness, and horror if you break off and pause before *rapid.*

Anne Boleyn is reported to have said, when in the Tower awaiting her beheading, something like this: " It shouldn't hurt very much. They say the executioner is skilful and I have such a little neck." To read the last seven words without a pause shows little imagination. A pause might be made in various places but the sentence seems to gain most in pathos and gruesomeness by a pause before *neck.*

But be careful not to let such pauses develop into what might be called the Soap-Opera-Stammer. So much first-time-ness can be gained by choking off a word and pausing as if to think of what to say next that this way of reading lines has become an outstanding mannerism of soap-opera delivery. At almost any hour of the morning you can tune in on something like this: "'Do you think—(choke)—Joan's other—(choke)—mother-in-law—(choke)—can ever—(choke)—forgive me?' 'Forgive? What is there to—(choke)—forgive?'"

RELATIVE EMPHASIS OF NOUNS AND ADJECTIVES

You probably remember from studying grammar that a noun is the name of a person or a thing, as arm, head, woman, story, New York, waiter, Frances, chair. And an adjective is a word that describes something, as true, funny, lovely, heavy. An adjective modifies a noun, a noun equivalent, or a pronoun, as true story, lovely woman, heavy chair. Sometimes a noun is used as an adjective to modify another noun, as boy baby, head waiter.

Since the noun amounts to being the name of the person or thing you are talking about, and since the adjective is merely a word that tells something about it, you might think that it would be logical and natural to emphasize the noun more than the adjective. But if you will listen to people talking, you may be surprised to notice how often they stress the adjective more than the noun. Of course, they do this spontaneously, without giving any thought to which of the words it is more reasonable to emphasize. But if you look at the constructions deliberately and logically, you will find that it is frequently more reasonable to stress the adjective. Yet most people in reading aloud tend to stress the noun more than the adjective, thereby producing an unnatural or reading-aloud effect.

Of course, you can't make any hard and fast rule about always stressing the adjective and subduing the noun. In this book we're concerned not with making rules, anyway, but with following principles.

Often you hear *seasons* stressed when someone reads Psalm 16:7. "I will bless the Lord, who hath given me counsel: my reins also instruct me in the night seasons." But stop and think of the real meaning. Whenever we're instructed, it's in some season, isn't it? But here we're reading about a certain special season: night seasons, contrasted, perhaps, with day seasons. Once you have thought of this, it will make you very uncomfortable to hear it read with the stress on the less meaningful word, *seasons.*

"She standeth in the top of high places, by the way in the places of the paths" (Proverbs 8:2). Which is more important in *high places,* the adjective or the noun? Aren't we always standing in some sort of place, if we're standing at all? The attention here is focused on high places, not low. You probably would never think of stressing the second *places* because you would stress the descriptive word, *paths.* Just so, it is natural to emphasize the other descriptive word, *high.*

"And the ruler of the synagogue answered with indignation, because that Jesus had healed on the sabbath day" (Luke 13:14). One wonders how anybody could read this with the stress on *day.* Yet it is often read that way, as though the ruler of the synagogue were objecting to his healing on the sabbath **day** rather than on the sabbath **night.** Of course, the implied contrast here is not between sabbath **day** and (implied) sabbath **night,** but between sabbath day and (implied) **week** day. So here is another place where logical thought requires emphasis on the adjective rather than on the noun.

In 1929 there was a play running on Broadway called *The Criminal Code.* Almost everybody who mentioned it called it The Criminal **Code,** as though it dealt with the criminal code rather than the criminal something else. Yet, if they hadn't just mechanically read the title aloud in that way, they would have seen that it was the criminal code, instead of the civil code or any other kind of code. The same is true of *The Philadelphia Story.*

Ridiculous meanings are often implied unconsciously when the word *man* is illogically stressed. In Psalm 37:23 we read of "the steps of a good man" as being "ordered by the Lord." If you stress *man,* it makes your readers infer that the steps of a good woman or of a good child are entirely different. It's not the fact that the individual is a man but the fact that he is good that is important. You almost always stress the adjective which modifies the word *man,* when it means merely an individual or a person in general.

This is true in the thirty-seventh verse of this same chapter, where we are told to " mark the perfect man." Doesn't this mean, not the perfect man as contrasted with the perfect woman, but the perfect man as contrasted with the imperfect man?

The little word *thing* is interesting to study. It is one of the most useful and versatile, as well as one of the vaguest, words in the English language, as you will see if you look at the dozen or more definitions in Webster's dictionary. Besides meaning an inanimate object, as distinguished from a person or from an intangible idea, it can mean whatever you are referring to—almost anything or almost nothing. It is a word of little character, with little significance of its own, and takes its meaning usually from the " thing " it refers to.

Res, the Latin word for *thing,* is usually given (in vocabularies) the general meaning of thing or affair. But students are taught to translate it as whatever is being talked about. So in almost any language *thing* is a word with little meaning in itself, just a stand-in or an understudy for some word with more character. In fact, you can usually leave out *thing* or *things* without changing the meaning, unless it is used in contrast with a person or an idea. Since this is so, is there, as a rule, any reason for emphasizing such a colorless word? Almost always it is the adjective modifying the word *thing* or *things* that carries the meaning.

Notice the words *anything, something, everything,* and *nothing.* In their ordinary use would you ever think of accenting the *-thing* parts of these words? No, we accent the colorful parts: *any, some, every,* and *no.*

But it's usually a different story when people begin to read aloud. In wordings like those in Matthew 17:11, " And Jesus answered and said unto them, Elias truly shall first come, and restore all things," many readers stress *things* instead of *all,* as though all things were contrasted with all people or all thoughts. Yet you could leave out *things* without changing the meaning one particle. In fact, in the Greek version of this verse, it is rendered simply πάντα (*panta*), *all* instead of πάντα τὰ χρήματα (*panta ta chremata*), *all things.* The word for *things* is not even expressed. The same would be true in Latin. It would be, not *omnes res* (*all things*), but simply *omnia* (*all*). Any word you can leave out without changing the meaning you need not and should not stress.

Suppose you said, " They will explain all things to us." You could have expressed the meaning as well by saying, " They will explain everything to us." Now you would never think of stressing *-thing* instead of *every-*, because *every-* is the meaningful part of the word.

The same reasoning that applies to *all things* applies to *these things* and *those things*. In Revelation 3:1 we read: " These things saith he that hath the seven Spirits of God." The Greek for these things is ταῦτα (*tauta*), *these*, instead of ταῦτα τὰ χρήματα (*tauta to chremata*), *these things*.

The soundness of the remarks about sometimes subduing such nouns as *men* and *things* is proved by the fact that *men* was not even expressed in the Greek from which Acts 21:28 was translated. When a word in the King James Version is found in italics, you are to understand that it was not expressed in the Greek but was supplied by the translator in English. Since the Greek was clear enough with the word omitted, the English would be, too. Of course, you won't omit it but you certainly don't need to stress it. " This is the man, that teacheth all men every where against the people."

In Psalm 107:43 *things* is italicized. " Whoso is wise, and will observe these things, even they shall understand the loving kindness of the Lord." The italics indicate that *things* was supplied by the translator. It could be omitted without changing or weakening the meaning.

Many of these nouns, besides *thing* or *things,* frequently have less meaning than the adjective modifying them. Among them are *points, places, times, conditions, phases, men,* etc.

Beware, however, of forming a thoughtless habit of stressing adjectives and subduing their nouns. This would be not only an annoying mannerism, but often a meaningless way of reading a passage. Many times the noun and not the adjective is the meaning-word.

> " Dreading the climax of all human ills,
> The inflammation of his weekly bills."

In these lines from Byron, wouldn't you stress the nouns, *ills* and *bills,* more than their adjectives, *human* and *weekly?* Try leaving out the adjectives. It doesn't change the meaning seriously, does it? **Any word you can leave out without changing the meaning you need not and should not stress.**

" He found him in a desert land, and in the waste howling wilderness." In Deuteronomy 32:10, *desert,* the adjective, carries more meaning than *land,* which really isn't necessary to the complete sense; but you certainly don't want to stress *waste* and *howling* more than *wilderness,* because *wilderness* itself has much meaning. *Wilderness* is a very colorful word, but *land,* as used here, has almost no color. (*Desert, waste,* and *howling* are used as adjectives in this sentence and *land* and *wilderness* are used as nouns.)

This is just a detail but it is worth noticing while we're thinking about nouns and their adjectives. Once in a while you will find a place where you shouldn't emphasize either one more than the other or you will imply an opposite that does not exist. If, for instance, you are reading something about " dying mortals," don't heavily stress *dying* and soft-pedal *mortals* or you will suggest that you mean to contrast dying mortals with undying mortals. Of course, there are no such things as undying mortals, because the word *mortal* actually means subject to death, since it comes from the Latin root word for *death, mort-.*

However, while you're taking care not to say **"dying** mortals," be sure that you don't fall into the opposite blunder of saying " dying **mortals,"** with no stress at all on *dying* and much on *mortals.* This would imply that there could be dying immortals, which is impossible, because the word *immortal* means not subject to death, as it comes from the same Latin word for *death* but has the Latin prefix, *im-* (or *in-*) which means *not.*

Then how shall you read such a construction? Without any emphasis at all? No; that would be not only difficult but meaningless. The natural and logical way to read such a construction is to stress the adjective and then to stress the noun a little more: **dying mortals.**

Watch carefully for constructions like these, as oral readers frequently bring out meanings in them that they don't intend to suggest at all.

" 'When I use a word,' Humpty Dumpty said in rather a scornful tone, 'it means just what I choose it to mean—neither more nor less.'

" 'The question is,' said Alice, 'whether you **can** make words mean different things.'

" 'The question is,' said Humpty Dumpty, ' which is to be master —that's all.'

" Alice was too much puzzled to say anything, so after a minute Humpty Dumpty began again. ' They've a temper, some of them— particularly verbs, they're the proudest—adjectives you can do anything with, but not verbs—however, I can manage the whole lot! ' "
—Lewis Carroll: *Through the Looking-Glass.*

Here is a construction to have a little fun with, if you are fond of words. Readers and speakers, except foreigners who are not quite at home in the English language, seldom make this mistake, but it is amusing to play with the following construction: In speaking of a **miniature** painter, we mean a painter of miniatures; by an **Italian** professor we mean a professor of the Italian language. But if we reverse the emphasis and speak of a miniature **painter** and an Italian **professor,** we mean a very small person who paints miniatures and a professor (of any subject) who is a native of Italy. See what happens when we reverse the usual emphasis in these expressions: living quarters, sick bed, sleeping car, giant killer, brief case, stumbling block, speeding ticket, milking machines, waiting room, parking meter, ground hog. You can go on making your own list. Who says proper emphasis isn't important?

PARENTHETICAL EXPRESSIONS

Most people understand that a parenthetical expression should be read in a much lower tone of voice than the rest of the sentence. This is true whether the parenthetical expression is set off by parentheses, by dashes, or by commas. (A parenthetical expression is something that is just thrown into the sentence, as an aside or an afterthought, more or less as this very sentence is thrown into this paragraph.) For example: " He was, I should say, about sixteen years old." "You have come to be—if I may say so—no longer necessary to our group." "We have found her to be (and I'm now quoting your favorite author) 'unlearned in the world's false subtleties.'"

The words set off by commas in the first sentence, by dashes in the second, and by parentheses in the third, are all parenthetical expressions and should be read in a lower tone of voice or "thrown away," as actors say. The implication is that the idea in each parenthetical expression is so well known or so unimportant that it need hardly be said.

Preposition with Personal Pronoun Object

If you have never paid special attention to the way people emphasize and pause in spontaneous conversation, you may not have noticed that, in many parts of the United States, when they use a preposition with a personal pronoun for its object, they frequently emphasize the word before the preposition, and then, a little less heavily, emphasize the preposition, but subdue the personal pronoun. Except under special circumstances, they seldom subdue the preposition and stress the pronoun. Therefore, you can frequently follow this pattern:

WHEN YOU READ A CONSTRUCTION CONTAINING A PREPOSITION WITH A PERSONAL PRONOUN FOR ITS OBJECT, STRESS THE WORD BEFORE THE PREPOSITION, PERHAPS STRESS THE PREPOSITION (SLIGHTLY LESS), AND SUBDUE THE PRONOUN.

If this suggestion sounds unnatural and mechanical to you, try the usual test of merely listening to people talk, and you will find that they generally stress the construction in this way. It is often possible to listen to a succession of story-tellers or speech-makers, supposed to be talking extemporaneously, and pick out, merely by their way of emphasizing this one construction, those who are really speaking spontaneously and those who are repeating something they have memorized.

Hearing his speech will be good for you.

Stress *good,* subduing *for* (the preposition), and stress (less heavily) *you* (the personal pronoun object of *for*). Notice how unnatural this sounds. A foreigner sometimes emphasizes this construction in this way, but one whose native language is English almost never does.

Now stress *good,* stress (less heavily) *for,* and subdue *you.* This is actually the way we often stress it, although in some sections of the country the word preceding the pronoun sometimes is not stressed.

The meaning of the word *pronoun* is a key to the reason why we unconsciously use this emphasis for this construction, when talking spontaneously. *Pro-* is a Latin prefix meaning *for* or *in place of.* A pronoun is a word that stands in the place of a noun. The implication of the noun that you are talking about is so obvious that you don't even repeat it; you use merely a substitute for it: a pronoun. You would never say, " Charlotte put on Charlotte's hat and told Charlotte's mother that Charlotte was going for a walk." After you have announced Charlotte the first time you don't keep on calling her name; you use the personal pronoun: " Charlotte put on her hat and told her mother that she was going for a walk." If the idea behind *her, her,* and *she* is so obvious or so unimportant that you can use a mere pronoun instead of a noun, then those three words certainly aren't important enough to stress.

Exceptions:

(1)   When the pronoun is contrasted with something. If you said, "I'll prepare dinner for you," you would stress according to the pattern given above, emphasizing *dinner,* and perhaps emphasizing *for* and subduing *you.* But if you said, " I'll prepare dinner for you but not for them," you would subdue *for* and stress *you* and *them,* because you would be making a contrast.

(2)   When the pronoun is followed by a restrictive modifier. (See Chapter V, Phrasing of Special Constructions, Restrictive and Nonrestrictive Modifiers.) In the sentence " This is a picture of him," you would usually stress *picture,* perhaps

stress (less heavily) *of,* and subdue *him* (unless you were contrasting *him* with someone else, meaning not him but her). For example, if you had been talking of a certain man and then said, " This is a picture of him," you would stress it as just suggested. But if you said, " This is a picture of him that we love," this way of emphasizing would not be the natural way and would sound clumsy and senseless. Because the personal pronoun, *him,* which is the object of the preposition, *of,* is followed by a restrictive modifier, *that we love,* we now subdue the preposition and stress the pronoun. We do this, not because somebody has made up a rule about it, but because it is the way we emphasize such a construction when using it spontaneously. When, in conversation, we end such a sentence with the pronoun we stress it one way; when we add a restrictive modifier we unconsciously change our way of stressing the whole sentence. This is done involuntarily by educated people who aren't thinking of restrictive modifiers and by uneducated people who may have never heard of one. So the sentence would be stressed thus: " This is a **picture** of **him** that we **love.**" Since *that we love* is a restrictive modifier, there is no pause between *him* and *that.*

(3) When the object of the pronoun is compound. " This is a picture of him and her " is read with the preposition subdued, and with *him* and *her,* the two objects, stressed. If you had said simply, " This is a picture of him," you would have stressed *picture,* perhaps stressed *of* (less heavily), and subdued *him* (unless you were contrasting *him* with someone else).

(4) When the word immediately preceding the preposition is a personal pronoun or some other word you would not normally stress. In the sentence, " Take it with you," you stress the preposition, *with,* as usual, and subdue the pronoun, *you,* as usual, but you do not follow the usual practice of emphasizing the word **immediately** preceding the preposition, as there is no reason to emphasize the word *it* here.

The same emphasis would be used in a sentence like this: " What has he with him? "

It may seem unnecessary to mention these exceptions, because not many people would read them in the wrong way. However, a few people are so anxious to apply the suggestion about subduing the personal pronoun object of a preposition that they have made a mechanical rule of it and rigidly apply it even in constructions like the four just discussed, even though their common sense should tell them it sounds unnatural and, therefore, wrong.

OVEREMPHASIS OF VERBS, ETC.

Some readers believe that because the verbs are the words that express action, stressing of verbs gives strength to their reading. You can't make a mechanical rule about which part of speech to emphasize; all you can do is to listen to people talk. When you do that, you will notice that often it is adjectives and nouns that receive stress rather than verbs. This warning does not mean that you should never stress a verb. Just avoid making a practice of deliberately hitting all the verbs for no special reason.

" And he came and touched the bier: and they that bare him stood still. And he said, Young man, I say unto thee, Arise." Try emphasizing all the verbs in Luke 7:14: *came, touched, bare, stood, said, say,* and *Arise.* It sounds forced. Now try some other arrangement of stress. One good way—but not the only good way—would be to stress the noun *bier* as much as *came* and *touched,* or perhaps more, and to stress the adjective *still* more than *bare* and *stood.* Of course, *Arise* is the climax and, therefore, should be stressed, but the noun *man* probably would be emphasized more than any of the other words in the sentence.

For no good reason, some readers stress almost every pronoun. Remember that you are not emphasizing either words or parts of speech; you are emphasizing ideas.

Exercises

(Do not just run through these casually. Absorb each point as you go. And work on just a few at a sitting.)

1. " Then enquired he of them the hour when he began to amend. And they said unto him, Yesterday at the seventh hour the fever left him " (John 4:52).

2. " And he trembling and astonished said, Lord, what wilt thou have me do? And the Lord said unto him, Arise, and go into the city, and it shall be told thee what thou must do" (Acts 9:6).

3. "Wisdom is the principal thing; therefore get wisdom: and with all thy getting get understanding " (Proverbs 4:7).

4. We must furnish relief for Europe and other famine-stricken regions.

5. " He said, ' What's time? leave Now for dogs and apes! Man has Forever.' "—Browning: *A Grammarian's Funeral.*

6. " They are upright as the palm tree, but speak not: they must needs be borne, because they cannot go. Be not afraid of them; for they cannot do evil, neither also is it in them to do good " (Jeremiah 10:5).

7. " And these three men, Shadrach, Meshach, and Abed-nego, fell down bound into the midst of the burning fiery furnace. Then Nebuchadnezzar the king was astonied, and rose up in haste, and spake, and said unto his counsellors, Did not we cast three men bound into the midst of the fire? They answered and said unto the king, True, O king. He answered and said, Lo, I see four men loose, walking in the midst of the fire, and they have no hurt; and the form of the fourth is like the Son of God " (Daniel 3:23–25).

8. We moth-proof your furs and mend the worn areas.

9. " These twelve Jesus sent forth, and commanded them, saying, Go not into the way of the Gentiles, and into any city of the Samaritans enter ye not " (Matthew 10:5).

10. " These in the robings of glory.
    Those in the gloom of defeat,
    All with the battle-blood gory,

In the dusk of eternity meet." —Finch: *The Blue and The Gray.*

11. "Enter ye in at the strait gate; for wide is the gate, and broad is the way, that leadeth to destruction, and many there be which go in thereat. Because strait is the gate, and narrow is the way, which leadeth unto life, and few there be that find it" (Matthew 7:13, 14).

12. "No lion shall be there, nor any ravenous beast shall go up thereon, it shall not be found there; but the redeemed shall walk there" (Isaiah 35:9).

13. York, I pray you, uncle, give me this dagger.
    Glou. My dagger, little cousin? with all my heart.
    Prince. A beggar, brother?
    York. Of my kind uncle, that I know will give . . .
    Glou. A greater gift than that I'll give my cousin.
    York. A greater gift! O, that's the sword to it.
    Glou. Ay, gentle cousin, were it light enough.
    York. O, then, I see you will part but with light gifts;
       In weightier things you'll say a beggar nay.
    —Shakespeare: *King Richard III:* Act III, Scene 1, lines 110–113, 115–119.

14. We hope this program will be enjoyed by lovers of opera and other forms of music.

15. ". . . to another prophecy; to another discerning of spirits; to another divers kinds of tongues; to another the interpretation of tongues . . ." (I Corinthians 12:10).

16. "For as by one man's disobedience many were made sinners, so by the obedience of one shall many be made righteous" (Romans 5:19).

17. There was good patronage of both movies and live shows.

18. "Now there are diversities of gifts, but the same Spirit. And there are differences of administrations, but the same Lord. And there are diversities of operations, but it is the same God which worketh all in all" (I Corinthians 12:4, 5, 6).

19. " For as in Adam all die, even so in Christ shall all be made alive " (I Corinthians 15:22).

20. " I will seek that which was lost, and bring again that which was driven away " (Ezekiel 34:16).

21. " But be not ye called Rabbi: for one is your Master, even Christ; and all ye are brethren " (Matthew 23:8).

22. The director was more considerate of professionals than they usually are of each other. a) Read this sentence stressing *usually* and subduing *each other*. What does it mean? Is the director a professional himself? b) Now read it slightly stressing *usually* but stressing *each other* still more strongly. What does it mean this time? Is the director a professional?

23. " And I say also unto thee, That thou art Peter, and upon this rock I will build my church; and the gates of hell shall not prevail against it " (Matthew 16:18).

24. " The lip of truth shall be established forever: but a lying tongue is but for a moment " (Proverbs 12:19).

25. Most policemen would rather prevent crime in their bailiwicks than make arrests.

26. " And yet thou art the nobler of us two:
What dare I dream of that thou canst not do? " Browning: *Any Wife to Any Husband.*

27. " And when the servant of the man of God was risen early, and gone forth, behold, an host compassed the city both with horses and chariots. And his servant said unto him, Alas, my master! how shall we do? " (II Kings 6:15).

28. a) " If any of you lack wisdom, let him ask of God, that giveth to all men liberally, and upbraideth not; and it shall be given him " (James 1:5).
b) " Wisdom is better than weapons of war." " If any of you lack wisdom, let him ask of God, that giveth to all men liberally, and upbraideth not; and it shall be given him " (Ecclesiates 9:18 and James 1:5).

29. "My little children, these things write I unto you, that ye sin not. And if any man sin, we have an advocate with the Father, Jesus Christ the righteous" (I John 2:1).

30. a) "Thou shalt have no other gods before me" (Exodus 20:3).
b) "And God spake all these words, saying, I am the Lord thy God, which have brought thee out of the land of Egypt, out of the house of bondage. Thou shalt have no other gods before me" (Exodus 20:1-3).

31. "He that dwelleth in the secret place of the most High shall abide under the shadow of the Almighty" (Psalm 91:1).

32. "And see if there be any wicked way in me, and lead me in the way everlasting" (Psalm 139:24).

33. Have you ever read *The Twelve-Pound Look* by Barrie?

34. "And call no man your father upon the earth: for one is your Father, which is in heaven" (Matthew 23:9).

35. "They that make a graven image are all of them vanity; and their delectable things shall not profit" (Isaiah 44:9).

36. "Tell ye, and bring them near; yea, let them take counsel together: who hath declared this from ancient time? who hath told it from that time?" (Isaiah 45:21).

37. The Declaration of Independence states that "all men are created equal."

38. "They shall take up serpents; and if they drink any deadly thing, it shall not hurt them" (Mark 16:18).

39. "And Jacob called unto his sons, and said, Gather yourselves together, that I may tell you that which shall befall you in the last days" (Genesis 49:1).

40. "They wandered in the wilderness in a solitary way" (Psalm 107:4).

41. "Therefore if any man be in Christ, he is a new creature: old things are passed away; behold, all things are become new" (II Corinthians 5:17).

42. " Through thy precepts I get understanding: therefore I hate every false way " (Psalm 119:104).

43. " I have declared the former things from the beginning; and they went forth out of my mouth, and I showed them; I did them suddenly, and they came to pass. . . . I have shewed thee new things from this time, even hidden things, and thou didst not know them " (Isaiah 48:3, 6).

44. " And when he came into the house, he suffered no man to go in, save Peter, and James, and John, and the father and the mother of the maiden " (Luke 8:51).

45. " For the invisible things of him from the creation of the world are clearly seen, being understood by the things that are made, even his eternal power and Godhead; so that they are without excuse " (Romans 1:20).

46. " The Duke (with the statue's face in the square)
Turned in the midst of his multitude
At the bright approach of the bridal pair."—Browning: *The Statue and the Bust.*

47. " Then off there flung in smiling joy,
And held himself erect
By just his horse's mane, a boy:
You hardly could suspect—
(So tight he kept his lips compressed,
Scarce any blood came through)
You looked twice ere you saw his breast
Was all but shot in two."—Browning: *Incident of the French Camp.*

48. " But that ye may know that the Son of man hath power on earth to forgive sins, (then saith he to the sick of the palsy,) Arise, take up thy bed, and go unto thine house " (Matthew 9:6).

49. That hat is very becoming to her.

50. " And he answered, Fear not: for they that be with us are more than they that be with them " (II Kings 6:16).

51. "He looked at her, as a lover can;
She looked at him, as one who awakes,—
The Past was a sleep and her life began."—Browning: *The Statue and the Bust.*

52. ". . . he hath sent me to bind up the brokenhearted, to proclaim liberty to the captives, and the opening of the prison to them that are bound" (Isaiah 61:1).

53. ". . . for he that cometh to God must believe that he is, and that he is a rewarder of them that diligently seek him" (Hebrews 11:6).

54. "And the nations of them which are saved shall walk in the light of it" (Revelation 21:24).

55. "For the eyes of the Lord run to and fro throughout the whole earth, to shew himself strong in the behalf of them whose heart is perfect toward him" (II Chronicles 16:9).

56. "Oh how great is thy goodness, which thou hast laid up for them that fear thee; which thou hast wrought for them that trust in thee before the sons of men!" (Psalm 31:19).

57. "The Lord is nigh unto them that are of a broken heart" (Psalm 34:18).

58. "O continue thy lovingkindness unto them that know thee" (Psalm 36:10).

59. ". . . after the image of him that created him . . ." (Colossians 3:10).

60. ". . . and the cries of them which have reaped are entered into the ears of the Lord of sabaoth" (James 5:4).

61. "But the Jews did not believe concerning him, that he had been blind, and received his sight, until they called the parents of him that had received his sight" (John 9:18).

62. "Behold, I am against them that prophesy false dreams" (Jeremiah 23:32).

63. ". . . all things are naked and opened unto the eyes of him with whom we have to do" (Hebrews 4:13).

64. ". . . And it was now dark, and Jesus was not come to them " (John 6:17).

65. ". . . Master, who did sin, this man, or his parents, that he was born blind? " (John 9:2).

66. "Daughter, be of good comfort; thy faith hath made thee whole " (Matthew 9:22).

67. "A little learning is a dangerous thing."—Pope: *Essay on Criticism.*

68. "We are fighting by ourselves alone, but we are not fighting for ourselves alone."—Winston Churchill.

69. "One God and Father of all, who is above all, and through all, and in you all " (Ephesians 4:6).

70. "And Abel, he also brought of the firstlings of his flock and of the fat thereof. And the Lord had respect unto Abel and to his offering: But unto Cain and to his offering he had not respect " (Genesis 4:4, 5).

71. "And there was war in heaven: Michael and his angels fought against the dragon; and the dragon fought and his angels " (Revelation 12:7).

72. Mrs. Lawrence soon called on us in our new apartment and made us feel very much at home. Several days later a young man knocked at our door and, when we opened it, smilingly said, " I'm Mr. Lawrence."

73. "So when they had dined, Jesus saith to Simon Peter, Simon, son of Jonas, lovest thou me more than these? He saith unto him, Yea, Lord; thou knowest that I love thee. He saith unto him, Feed my lambs.
"He saith unto him again the second time, Simon, son of Jonas, lovest thou me? He saith unto him, Yea, Lord; thou knowest that I love thee. He saith unto him, Feed my sheep.
"He saith unto him the third time, Simon, son of Jonas, lovest thou me? Peter was grieved because he said unto him the third time, Lovest thou me? And he said unto him, Lord, thou

knowest all things; thou knowest that I love thee" (John 21: 15–17).

ANSWER BOOK

These so-called "answers" are really only suggestions which you may accept or reject as your reason dictates. And surely no one will misunderstand the suggestions about leaving out certain words without altering the sense. There is no intention of suggesting that you irreverently tamper with the meaning in any way, especially in reading the Bible verses. And of course there is no intention of intimating that you should leave out the words when actually reading the verses aloud.

1. John 4:52. Since the question contained the word *hour,* surely the servant, in answering, subdued *hour* and emphasized *seventh,* the new or contrasting idea, telling which hour. Suppose someone should ask you, "At what time of day did it happen?" Would you reply, "At noontime"? Surely you would say, "At **noontime**." (New and Old Ideas.)

2. Acts 9:6. Although this is frequently read with some stress on *what thou must do,* doesn't this just clutter the meaning? *What thou must do* is merely a repetition of *what wilt thou have me do* and, therefore, should not be emphasized. For practice, try reading the verse leaving out the last four words and you will see that the sense does not lose anything really essential, because the reader is not tempted to devote his attention to unimportant words and, therefore, can attend to the important ideas: going into the city, and being told. (New and Old Old Ideas.)

3. Proverbs 4:7. The first *wisdom* here is always stressed, naturally; but the second *wisdom* has become an old idea and, therefore, is soft-pedaled so that the new idea, *get,* may be emphasized. In the third clause, *getting* now has become an old idea; so both *getting* and *get* are subdued and the new idea, the

climax of the verse, *understanding,* is brought out. (New and Old Ideas.)

4. Europe is a region; further, it is a famine-stricken region; therefore, both *famine-stricken* and *regions* should be subdued, as old ideas implied in *Europe.* The new idea is *other.* (Implied Contrast.)

5. *Now, dogs, apes, Man,* and *Forever* should be stressed. This is a double contrast, *Now* with *Forever,* and *Man* with *dogs* and *apes.* (Double Contrast.)

6. Jeremiah 10:5. Naturally you will stress *evil,* and *good* is the only other word from there on that needs emphasis, since *neither also is it in them to do* is just another way of saying *they cannot do.* If you left out *also is it in them to do,* wouldn't it still make sense? **Any word that you can leave out without changing the meaning you certainly need not and should not stress.** (New and Old Ideas. Simple Contrast.)

7. Daniel 3:23, 24, 25. This is an excellent example of double contrast. In verse 23, *three* and *bound* may be stressed but not heavily. In verse 24 is good proof that we stress because of ideas and not because of words: the principle of subduing old ideas would suggest subduing *three* and *bound* in verse 24, since they are repetitions from 23. In reality, however, they should be stressed, because mentally Nebuchadnezzar is contrasting them with *four* and *loose,* although he does not actually say *four* and *loose* until verse 25. (Double Contrast.)

8. This sentence from a radio commercial was read with the stress on *areas.* But the unworn places as well as the worn are areas; therefore, *areas* should be thrown away as an old idea and *worn* should be stressed because of its contrast with implied *unworn.* (Implied Contrast.)

9. Matthew 10:5. Frequently this is read with the heaviest emphasis on the very last word. But *enter ye not* means exactly the same as *go not into.* Paraphrase it: Enter ye not into the way of the Gentiles, and into any city of the Samaritans enter

ye not. Now, don't you naturally stress *Samaritan* (new idea, contrasted with *Gentiles*) and soft-pedal *enter ye not?* Then *enter ye not* should be subdued even when you read it in its correct wording, the last emphasis falling on *Samaritans.* If you entirely left out *enter ye not,* the meaning would be still fairly clear. (Implied Synonym.)

10. The first two lines contain a double contrast, *These* with *Those,* and *glory* with *defeat.* Don't stress *These* and *glory* as hard as *Those* and *defeat,* however. (Remember you don't have to wave a flag to make your hearers realize that you know where the emphasis belongs and to make them realize the sense of the passage.) (Double Contrast.)

11. Matthew 7:13, 14. *Strait* is a word that was used in Biblical times to mean the same as narrow. They are synonyms. Then wouldn't the following be the truly logical way to read these two verses? The *wide* should be stressed, being contrasted with the first *strait;* the second *gate* subdued (old idea). *Broad* should be subdued (same idea as *wide*) and *way* stressed (slightly contrasted with *gate*). In verse 14, *strait* should be stressed (contrasted with *wide* in verse 13) and then *gate* should be subdued (same idea as second *gate* in verse 13). *Narrow,* although frequently read with emphasis, should really be soft-pedaled, as it means almost exactly the same as *strait.* *Way,* in verse 14, should be slightly stressed, as contrasted with *gate.* Of course, *life* is contrasted with *destruction* and *few* with *many.*

If you will practice these verses, substituting *narrow* for its synonym, *strait,* and *broad* for its synonym, *wide,* I think you will agree that the suggestion above is the really logical way to read these words discussed. But this still does not mean that everyone will read these verses alike: most people emphasize *find* and subdue *it,* at the end of verse 14. This is perfectly satisfactory reading. Someone else may lightly subdue *find* and heavily stress *it,* contrasting *it* (the narrow way, which **few** find) with *thereat* (the **wide** way, which **many** find or go in at). Either of these last two readings is sensible. Neither is

" wrong." (New and Old Ideas, Double Contrast; Implied Synonyms).

12. Isaiah 35:9. *Lion* is the important idea. The next word that is usually stressed by readers is *beast*. But isn't a lion a beast? Then *beast* is an old idea, meaning the same as *lion*. When this is pointed out to people, usually they next read it emphasizing *ravenous*. But isn't a lion a ravenous beast? Then *ravenous beast* together mean about the same as *lion*. Then what word will you stress? *Any* brings out a contrast with *lion,* since a lion is not just any ravenous beast but one special kind. Stressing *any* implies that you mean neither a lion nor any other ravenous beast. (New and Old Ideas; Simple Contrast.)

13. Shakespeare: *King Richard III*. Act III, Scene 1, lines 110–113, 115–119. When you practice reading material written in archiac language, like parts of the Bible or of Shakespeare, or material which is very complicated and compact, like Browning's poems, it is often a good idea to reword or paraphrase them into modern language, to put them into your own words. Practice with this very unliterary rewording of Shakespeare's lines:

York. I beg you, uncle, give me this dagger.
Glou. I give you my dagger, little cousin, with all my heart.
Prince. Are you a beggar, brother?
York. I am a beggar of my kind uncle, who I know will give to me.
Glou. A greater gift than that I'll give my cousin.
York. A greater gift! Oh, that's the sword that matches it.
Glou. Yes, gentle cousin, if it were light enough.
York. Oh, then, I see you will part with only light gifts;
    In weightier things you will say no to a beggar.

In writing to little Isa Bowman, his young friend who played the part of York, Lewis Carroll gave this helpful criticism of her emphasis in this scene: " Would your Highness like me to go on calling you the Duke of York, or shall I say ' My own darling Isa'? . . . Now I'm going to find fault with my pet about her acting. What's the good of an old uncle like me except to find fault? You do the meeting with the Prince of Wales very nicely and lovingly; and in teasing your uncle for his dagger and sword, you are very sweet and playful; and—'but that's not finding fault!' Isa says to herself. Isn't it? Well, I'll try again. Didn't I hear you say, 'In weightier things you'll say a beggar nay,' leaning on the word 'beggar'? If so, it was a mistake. My rule for knowing which word to lean on is the word that tells you something new, something that is different from what you expected. . . ."—Florence Becker Lennon: *Victoria Through the Looking-Glass.** It seems most unlikely that anyone, especially a trained young actress, could have made such a blunder as stressing *beggar* in line 119, even though one has to go all the way back to line 112 to realize that *beggar* is an old idea. Obviously, *nay,* the contrast, is the word to emphasize and *beggar* the word to slight, in line 119, because in line 111 Gloucester has said the beggar *yes* and in line 119 he is saying the beggar *no.* (New and Old Ideas.)

14. The natural way to speak or read this sentence seems so apparent that it is hard to believe that a famous music critic read it recently on the radio with the stress on *music.* (He was supposed to be not reading aloud at all but just saying it during a supposedly unrehearsed, spontaneous interview; but his stressing of *music* gave away the fact that he was reading a prepared script, since nobody just speaking—that is, **thinking** —this sentence for the first time would ever emphasize *music.* This sentence is rather similar to Ex. 12. Isn't opera music? Then don't stress *music,* because it's an old idea. Then shall you stress *forms?* No, because opera is a form of music. Then don't emphasize *forms,* another old idea. Stress *other,* because it brings out the contrast between *opera* (one form of music) and other forms of music. (New and Old Ideas; Simple Contrast.)

15. I Corinthians 12:10. You will probably emphasize the first *tongues* as a new idea; but see how preposterous it sounds to

* Published by Simon and Schuster, Inc., New York.

stress the second *tongues* instead of subduing it as an old idea and stressing the new, *interpretation*. (New and Old Ideas.)

16. Romans 5:19. The double contrast here is between *disobedience* and *obedience* and between *sinners* and *righteous*. Again, *obedience* and *righteous* are more heavily stressed than the first two contrasted words. Do not stress *dis-* too much but accent *disobedience* naturally, on the third syllable, since accenting *dis-* would be looking forward too much and would be too obvious. But if *obedience* preceded *disobedience* then it would be natural to accent *dis-*, as in the illustration given in paragraph 13 of Chapter II. (Double Contrast.)

17. A war commentator stressed *shows* in a sentence similar to this, but aren't movies shows, too? They are "canned" shows, in contrast to plays or revues, which are "live." So he should logically have leaned on *live* and slighted *shows*. (Implied Contrast.)

18. The key words are: *diversities, gifts, same,* and *Spirit*. To emphasize any others detracts from these. *Administrations*, being slightly contrasted with *gifts*, needs emphasis, but *differences*, being almost a synonym of *diversities* although not the same word, needs subduing. The second *same* is an old idea. In the third sentence, *diversities* is old again and *operations*, although very similar in meaning to *administrations*, is the nearest thing to a new idea in the first clause, and you can hardly read a whole clause without something to tack a little emphasis on. (Remember the frightened passenger who completed his first airplane ride much relieved and said, "But I never put my whole weight down the entire time.") (Implied Synonyms; New and Old Ideas; Simple Contrast.)

19. The double contrast is brought out by stressing *Adam* and *Christ, die* and *alive,* is it not? (Double Contrast.)

20. Readers of this verse frequently emphasize *lost* and *away*. But thoughtful analysis will reveal that, although *lost* should be emphasized, *away* should not, being an old idea. The word *away* has not been expressed before but the idea of away-ness

is implied in *lost,* which means something like strayed-away. So, if you subdue *away* and stress *driven,* don't you obtain a new and legitimate light on the meaning of this verse, by showing a contrast between being merely strayed away and actually driven away? (Implied Contrast or Implied Synonyms.)

21. If you look up the word *Rabbi* you will find that it means Master. Therefore, shouldn't you stress *one* and subdue *Master?* You might even stress second *ye.* This brings out the otherwise hidden meaning that *Rabbi* means *Master,* because subduing *Master* implies that *Master* is an old idea. Therefore, it must mean the same as *Rabbi.* (Implied Synonyms.)

22. a) If you subdue *each other* it would suggest that *each other* is an old idea, echoing *professionals,* and imply that the director himself is a professional. (Implied New and Old Ideas.)
    b) If you stress *each other* you suggest that it is a new idea and, therefore, contrasted with *professionals.* So your hearers infer that the director is not a professional. Moral: Unless you read in a complete monotone, you are going to convey, by your emphasis, some meaning or other, either the right one or the wrong one. (Implied New and Old Ideas.)

23. Peter is Πέτρος in Greek, the same as πέτρος, which means a rock. In this verse, therefore, *rock* is really an old idea, meaning the same as *Peter.* If you think it would not be too startling to your hearers you can imply this by stressing *Peter,* subduing *rock* (old idea), and stressing *upon* (new idea or contrast). (Implied Synonyms.)

24. Does stressing *tongue* bring out the meaning here? Rather, shouldn't *tongue* be subdued as an old idea? Of course, *tongue* doesn't mean exactly the same as *lip,* but they are considered similar in meaning here, both being organs of speech. *Lying* should be emphasized, to contrast with *truth.* (Implied Synonyms.)

25. One oral reader of this sentence stressed *bailiwicks* and *arrests.* There is no contrast between these two ideas, but there is a

contrast between preventing crime and making arrests. Therefore, stress *prevent* and *arrests*. (Simple Contrast.)

26.   *I* is contrasted with *thou* and *dream* with *do*. (Double Contrast.)

27.   Here is where many readers miss the carry-over right in the
same verse. They emphasize the second *servant;* but it's the
same one they've just been talking about and, therefore, should
be thrown away. (New and Old Ideas.)

28.   a) Suppose you are reading a list of Bible verses about
wisdom. If James 1:5 is the first on the list you will naturally
stress *wisdom*.
b) But if it has been immediately preceded by, for example,
the first part of Ecclesiastes 9:18 ("Wisdom is better than
weapons of war") you will naturally subdue the *wisdom* in the
verse from James and stress *lack*. (Carry-over.)

29.   If you read the second sentence of this verse by itself, surely
you would stress *sin,* introduced for the first time. But if you
read the whole verse in order, wouldn't stressing *if* (new idea)
and subduing the second *sin* (old idea) bring out the sense of
"if any man does sin?" (Carry-over.)

30.   a) This book does not attempt to "interpret" the First Commandment. Virtually everyone reads it meaningfully, stressing
gods and *me*. Most stress *no* and some stress *other,* quite
logically. This uniformity of reading is due partly to the fact
that it is generally read without the two introductory verses.
b) For an experiment, read the first three verses of Exodus 20
in their normal order. In both the first two verses *God* is the
central idea. Therefore, in verse three *gods* is an old idea
(although not synonymous with *God,* of course) and *me* is an
old idea. Then the way to read it under these circumstances
is to subdue *gods* and stress *other* and *before*. Perhaps, however, you have never heard it read this way, even following the
first two verses, as the usual reading has become very firmly
crystallized in our thought and very few readers ever think of
the carry-over here. (Carry-over.)

31. Don't we assume that we're always in some sort of place? Then isn't the **kind** of place (*secret*) the important word? (Relative Emphasis of Nouns and Adjectives.)

32. It is interesting and illuminating to notice the way **this** is generally read. Exchange the places of the last two words and then read it aloud, with *everlasting* preceding *way*. Many readers, if it were written in this form, would follow the usual, natural pattern and automatically soft-pedal the two nouns (*way*), stressing the adjectives (*wicked* and *everlasting*). This is a more sensible reading, since *everlasting* is a more important idea than *way;* also, *wicked* has more meaning than *way.* (Nouns and Adjectives.)

33. This famous play is almost always referred to as " The Twelve-Pound **Look**," an emphasis that conveys no idea of its meaning. It is the story of a woman who wanted to earn twelve pounds (in English money) and whose look, or expression, betrayed the fact. You wouldn't say someone has a self-conscious **look**; you'd say she has a **self-conscious** look, wouldn't you? So this woman has a **twelve-pound** look, not a twelve-pound **look**. (Nouns and Adjectives.)

34. This is sometimes read with the emphasis on *man*. Remember that when you stress a word you often imply a contrast with its opposite, whether you intend to or not. Here, if you stress *man*, you imply a contrast with *woman*, which you surely do not mean to do. *No* is decidedly the important thought here, as *man* could be omitted entirely without ruining the sense by replacing *no man* with *nobody, no one*, or simply *none*. (Nouns and Adjectives.)

35. Isn't *delectable* more meaningful than *things?* (Nouns and Adjectives.)

36. Do you mean " from ancient **time** "? Don't you mean rather " from **ancient** time " as differing from " from **present** time," perhaps? (Nouns and Adjectives.)

37. How many times have you heard school children (and adults) say that " all **men** are created equal "? Aren't the women

created equal, too? If you leave out *men* altogether, you have not changed the sense. **Any word that you can leave out without changing the sense you need not and should not stress.** (Nouns and Adjectives.)

38. This verse contains an especially interesting instance of the logic of subduing the word *thing*. It is frequently read with the emphasis placed illogically on *thing* instead of on *deadly*. But reverse the order and read it " anything deadly." Notice that now you wouldn't think of emphasizing *thing;* you naturally emphasize *deadly,* the word that carries the meaning. (Nouns and Adjectives.)

39. Is it " last **days** " or " last days "? In other words, is it contrasting last days with last nights or last days with these days? (Nouns and Adjectives.)

40. Wherever they wandered, it was in some sort of way, wasn't it? Then doesn't this mean " a **solitary** way "? (Nouns and Adjectives.)

41. Do you mean " any **man** "? What about women and children? (Nouns and Adjectives.)

42. Is it " false **way** " or " false way "? (Nouns and Adjectives.)

43. Aren't *former, new,* and *hidden* more important than *things?* (Nouns and Adjectives.)

44. If you stress *man,* as some readers do, you imply that perhaps women but no men were allowed to go in. (Nouns and Adjectives.)

45. There is no more reason for emphasizing the first *things* than the second *things. Invisible* and *that are made* carry the thought. (Nouns and Adjectives.)

46. Lower your voice to read *with the statue's face in the square.* (Parenthetical Expressions.)

47. Break off abruptly after *suspect;* then lower your voice for the words in parentheses. (Parenthetical Expressions.)

48. This parenthetical expression is usually read in the logical way,

so far as emphasis is concerned, but is generally phrased incorrectly, being read with what precedes instead of with what follows. The first seventeen words of this verse were said mainly to the scribes; it was the last ten that were said to the sick of the palsy. Therefore, shouldn't you separate the parenthetical expression from the first seventeen words by a long pause and connect it with the last ten by pausing hardly at all between them? (Parenthetical Expressions.)

49. Doesn't stressing *becoming,* stressing (less heavily) *to,* and subduing *her,* sound more natural than stressing *becoming,* stressing (less heavily) *her,* and subduing *to?* (Preposition with Personal Pronoun Object.)

50. If this said, " they that be with us are more than they that be against us," you would emphasize *with* and *against* and subdue each *us.* But since the contrast is not between *with* and *against* but between *us* and *them,* you subdue the preposition *with* each time and stress the personal pronoun objects, *us* and *them.* (Preposition with Personal Pronoun Object.)

51. If you were reading " She looked at him " by itself you would probably stress *looked,* slightly stress the preposition *at,* and subdue its personal pronoun object *him,* as you would in conversation. But because here *at him* is contrasted with *at her* in the preceding line, you obviously would emphasize *him* (and *she*) and slight *at.* In the preceding line you might also stress *He* and *her,* subduing *at,* to bring out the same contrast; however, to avoid obviousness and overemphasis and to achieve the quality of first-time-ness it might be more effective to emphasize it just as if you didn't know what was coming in the next line, by not giving special emphasis to *He,* by stressing *looked,* by stressing (less heavily) *at,* and soft-pedaling *her.* (Preposition with Personal Pronoun Object; Carry-over; First-time-ness.)

52. If this ended with the *them* and if *that are bound* were not expressed, you would naturally stress *prison* and *to* and subdue *them.* But *that are bound* is a restrictive modifier of *them.* So you subdue *to,* stress *them,* and make no pause between *them*

and *that are bound.* (Preposition with Personal Pronoun Object.)

53. Subdue *of,* stress *them,* and make no pause between *them* and its restrictive modifier, *that diligently seek him.* (Preposition with Personal Pronoun Object.)

54. Subdue *of,* stress *them,* and make no pause between *them* and its restrictive modifier, *which are saved.* (Preposition with Personal Pronoun Object.)

55. Subdue *of,* stress *them,* and make no pause between *them* and its restrictive modifier, *whose heart is perfect toward him.* (Preposition with Personal Pronoun Object.)

56. Subdue first *for,* stress first *them,* and make no pause between first *them* and its restrictive modifier, *that fear thee;* subdue second *for,* stress second *them,* and make no pause between second *them* and its restrictive modifier, *that trust in thee before the sons of men!* (Preposition with Personal Pronoun Object.)

57. Subdue *unto,* stress *them,* and make no pause between *them* and its restrictive modifier, *that are of a broken heart.* (Preposition with Personal Pronoun Object.)

58. Subdue *unto,* stress *them,* and make no pause between *them* and its restrictive modifier, *that know thee.* (Preposition with Personal Pronoun Object.)

59. Subdue *of,* stress *him,* and make no pause between *him* and its restrictive modifier, *that created him.* (Preposition with Personal Pronoun Object.)

60. Subdue *of,* stress *them,* and make no pause between *them* and its restrictive modifier, *which have reaped.* (Preposition with Personal Pronoun Object.)

61. Stress *believe,* stress less heavily *concerning,* and subdue *him,* since there is no restrictive modifier following. But subdue *of,* stress second *him,* and make no pause between second *him* and its restrictive modifier, *that had received his sight.* (Preposition with Personal Pronoun Object.)

62. Stress *them,* because it is followed by a restrictive modifier, *that prophesy false dreams.* Ordinarily you would not heavily stress *against,* the preposition of which *them* is the object; but because *am* is a weak word and there is no particular reason for stressing *I* in this sentence, and because you have to hang your emphasis somewhere, *against* is the only other candidate for stress. (Preposition with Personal Pronoun Object.)

63. No, you don't stress *unto* and subdue *eyes,* because *eyes* is a noun and not a personal pronoun. For some strange reason, this odd way of emphasizing is used in conversation only when the object of the preposition is a personal pronoun. What we are concerned with in this verse is subduing *of* and stressing *him,* because *him* is followed by a restrictive modifier, *with whom we have to do.* (Preposition with Personal Pronoun Object.)

64. Since there is no restrictive modifier following *them,* just emphasize *come,* emphasize (less heavily) *to,* and subdue *them.* (Preposition with Personal Pronoun Object.)

65. With probably some vague idea that there is a contrast between *this* and an implied *that,* many stress *this* and *parents.* But this suggests the thought of **this** man and **that** man, implying that his **parents** were " **that** man." The contrast really is between *man* and *parents,* which are the words to stress. (Simple Contrast.)

66. Frequently *whole* is emphasized as much as *faith* and sometimes even more. But *hath made thee whole* is, by implication, an old idea. It was apparent that she was whole and the new idea was the **reason** for her being whole: her faith. So *faith* might be emphasized and *hath made thee whole* subdued. (Implied New and Old Ideas.)

67. *Dangerous* is more important than *thing.* You could leave out *a* and *thing* and the sense would remain. (Nouns and Adjectives.)

68. These magnificent words certainly deserve to be read with first-time-ness. If you read them in the obvious way, emphasiz-

ing *by* to contrast later with *for,* you cause your hearers to be anticipating something that is coming and you deprive them of the full effect of the first six words. Surely it would be better to read up to the comma as though you weren't going to say another word. You would emphasize *ourselves* and *alone* and use a falling inflection on *alone.* Then, when the impression has been made, you could read the rest, stressing *not* and *for.* (First-time-ness.)

69. This verse is similar to Romans 11:36, which is seldom read with the desirable first-time-ness. It would be no worse to emphasize *of* in this verse than to stress *of* in the verse from Romans; yet readers usually give **this** verse first-time-ness, by subduing *of* and stressing *all,* and then stressing *above, through,* and *in* and subduing the last three *all's.* (First-time-ness.)

70. The contrast here is so clear that many Bible-readers show it too soon, thus losing first-time-ness by anticipating. If you slightly emphasize the second *Abel* and the first *offering,* you let the main ideas of this clause come out; but if you heavily emphasize the second *his,* subduing the first *offering,* you make it too clear that you are going to talk about somebody else and **his** offering. First let your hearers get the idea of the way Abel and his **offering** were received; then bring in Cain and **his** offering. You can do this by lightly emphasizing the second *Abel* and the first *offering,* subduing the second *his* and the second *offering,* and more heavily emphasizing *Cain* and the third *his.* (First-time-ness.)

71. This is a construction similar to the one just discussed. *Michael* and the first *angels* are the important ideas. You haven't recently been reading about Michael and his angels and so naturally you would give them some stress as new ideas. If you subdue the first *angels* and stress the first *his* you indicate that in just a minute you will mention someone else and **his** angels. This would not have first-time-ness. So you should slightly emphasize *Michael* and the first *angels,* subdue the first *his* and the second *angels* and stress *dragon* and the second *his.* (First-time-ness.)

72. Which words did you emphasize in the quotation? *I* and *Mr.?* Mrs. Lawrence has just been mentioned and so there is a contrast between *Mrs. Lawrence* and *I,* and there is also a contrast between *Mrs. Lawrence* and *Mr. Lawrence.* True, but those contrasts are in the thought of the reader but probably not in the thought of the speaker of the quotation, Mr. Lawrence. The reader must read those three words as Mr. Lawrence said them, as he thought them. The reader is thinking that Mrs. Lawrence was mentioned in the preceding sentence. But the speaker of the three words probably wasn't thinking, "Mrs. Lawrence was here several days ago and now I am here: **Mr. Lawrence.**" He was thinking merely: "**I** am Mr. **Lawrence.**" It would be a very alert reader who would be able to read a passage like this at sight with logical emphasis. (First-time-ness.)

73. We do not dramatize or emotionalize the Bible if we read it with real reverence and good taste. Still, direct conversation in the Bible must be read with natural inflections or it will not even make sense. Hence, the question in verse 15 would naturally be read with a rising inflection, as it expects a yes-or-no answer. It would be read in a life-like manner, since it is a direct quotation. This is true of the question in verse 16 also, and of the same question quoted directly in verse 17. But look at " Peter was grieved because he said unto him the third time, Lovest thou me? " The question in this case is no longer a direct quotation. It is a quotation of a direct quotation. The three words, *Lovest thou me?* could actually be replaced with the pronoun *it* by slightly rearranging the sentence: Peter was grieved because he said it unto him the third time. Any word that can be omitted—or replaced with a pronoun—without altering the sense, you need not emphasize and you need not inflect vividly. So you can slightly subdue *Lovest thou me?* and read it with a level or only a slightly rising inflection.

Paraphrasing implies no disrespect to these Bible verses. Often it is the best way to arrive at the meaning of a passage written in the language of King James' day. (First-time-ness.)

SHOULD WE TRY TO READ A PASSAGE DIFFERENTLY EVERY TIME?

Sometimes someone applying these principles will find that a sentence which has been almost always read in one certain way should logically be stressed or phrased quite differently. Perhaps he may feel that this new reading, once discovered, is the only logical way and that no carry-over would ever change it. Someone else may then protest, "But then everyone would read it exactly alike!" To which I always feel like replying, "So what! They all read it alike and **don't** bring out the meaning! What's so awful about always reading this particular sentence the same way and **bringing** out the meaning?"

Some readers feel that a sentence should be read a different way each time. They feel that this preserves spontaneity. But ask yourself: Does the **meaning** change every time? Unless the meaning itself changes (and it well may do so, from carry-over) how can the phrasing and emphasis which convey the meaning change? Of course, as we have seen, there may be several ways to read one sentence to bring out several logical meanings. The reader takes his choice; or he may use one reading one time and another the next, if he considers them equally sound. But, if you find a sentence in which the meaning never varies and if you conclude that there is just one way to bring out this meaning, how can you change your reading?

This policy of changing a reading each time just for the sake of change can produce labored and fantastic readings, and often brings out a misleading implication.

IV

INTRODUCTION TO PHRASING

THE WHOLE PURPOSE of this chapter is to help you to phrase naturally, as in conversation.

A phrase is a group of related words that conveys a thought.
Almost every sentence contains one phrase or more, and after some
of these the reader should pause.

A PHRASE IS A GROUP OF RELATED WORDS THAT
CONVEYS A THOUGHT.

A PAUSE IS A SHORT PERIOD OF SILENCE THAT FOL-
LOWS A SPOKEN WORD OR PHRASE.

A phrase serves three purposes. Its first and most obvious function
is to give the reader an opportunity to breathe. In conversation we
breathe comfortably and frequently without even thinking about it,
because we breathe at the natural phrasing places, that is, at the
ends of ideas. But sometimes an unpracticed reader fails to breathe
at the natural place and then finds himself having to stop for breath
at a most inappropriate point.

The second function of the phrase is to give the reader an opportunity to look ahead to see what he is to read next. During the pause
following the first phrase he is not only taking a new breath, if he
needs to, but also quickly scanning the sentence to the end of the
next small thought. Then he reads that thought aloud, then pauses
to look ahead through the next phrase, and then reads it in turn.

In a way, pauses are almost as important as the words. Sydney
Smith said of Macaulay: " [He] has occasional flashes of silence
which make his conversation perfectly delightful."

The first two functions of the phrase or the pause are for the
benefit of the reader; the third is for the audience's benefit: the

audience hears the reader, or grasps his meaning, during his "flashes of silence" instead of while he is speaking. The audience must be given these frequent opportunities to catch up with the reader's meaning and think about it or they will be left hopelessly behind. If the reader never paused except at the end of each sentence, his audience would still be pondering the first part of the sentence while he was reading the last word of it. As a rule, the more experienced a reader or a speaker is, the more pauses he uses, especially if the audience is large or the acoustics poor.

Have you ever had someone ask you a question when you weren't paying attention and then, during a moment of silence when you were about to ask to have the question repeated, seemed actually to hear an echo of it and been able to answer it? That illustrates to some extent how your audience "hears" you during your pauses.

Not only does the pause help to bring out the meaning; a well-placed pause sometimes heightens the effect of a reading as nothing else could. It has been said that sometimes a period of silence is the most beautiful part of a musical selection. One of the loveliest moments in *Lucia di Lammermoor* is the quivering silence preceding the orchestral introduction to the great Sextette.

And one of the most difficult things for an inexperienced reader or actor to do is just to pause: to be still; to inhale, perhaps; and to look ahead.

Sometimes the director of a play who is having difficulty in getting an actor to pause tells him to count three silently after a certain word and to count ten after another.

It is judicious phrasing that helps to make a good sight reader. After conscientious practice of the following principles of phrasing, many readers have found that they could read passages at sight better than they could have before after hours of haphazard practice. "I have to practice more than most pianists, because I have almost no technique," says Percy Grainger, quoted in *The New Yorker* by Robert Lewis Taylor.

Webster's New International Dictionary, Second Edition, defines the verb *to phrase* as "to pronounce in sense groups." (It is interesting that the noun is defined as "a breath group.") There are many types of "sense group" and there can be no cut-and-dried rule about when to pause after such a group, since good oral reading is not merely a science but also an art. Therefore, it is a good idea for the reader to learn all, or most of, the places at which a pause can be made and then decide for himself which possible pauses he wants or needs to use.

Different persons reading the same sentence naturally will choose different places to pause. Six clever milliners, each bent on creating a sailor hat, will use the same principles of design but each will apply them in her own way and the six hats will vary in color, material, and shape, and yet each will be effective; six skilled readers may phrase a paragraph six different ways and yet all will make clear the basic meaning.

Perhaps the strongest and most prevalent misconception about phrasing is that a good reader must pause for every comma. It would be hard to think of anything farther from the truth. If you have supposed this practice to be advisable or if you have been taught this misconception, the first thing to do is to realize *why* it is not a sound practice. You must be completely convinced that the premises on which you proceed are sound or you will not apply them willingly and well.

First, in reading aloud, you are merely trying to reproduce the way you would say the same words in spontaneous conversation. You are trying to " be natural." But deliberately to be natural is about the most difficult task you can attempt.

Haven't you known persons who, when placed before a camera and told to " look natural," immediately look unnatural and strained? They become self-conscious and can't remember how they look and feel when they " look natural." Just so, an inexperienced reader, placed before an audience or a microphone and told to " read naturally," has no idea how he would say the same words if he were just talking them as they came to his thought.

In conversation we don't always pause where a grammarian would place the commas. If you have a keen ear for sound and for grammatical constructions and will listen carefully to the way people talk, you will concede that this is true.

Second, some of our most effective writers do not always punctuate according to the rules of grammar. This is acknowledged to be true of many writers, from Shakespeare through Dickens to some of our most highly ranked novelists and essayists of the present day. It is quite possible to find errors in grammar and punctuation in recognized grammars and dictionaries, if one has nothing better to do than to look for them. Remember the old story about the text on grammar which said that " a preposition should never be used to end a sentence with." It would be possible to compile a volume entitled *Bad Grammar in Good Books.*

Of course, it is much easier to learn the rules of grammar and punctuation than to create a literary masterpiece. As Bertrand Russell says, " There is no point whatever in being able to spell anything. Shakespeare and Milton could not spell. Marie Corelli and Alfred Austin could." * But the fact that you cannot always rely on an author's punctuation is an argument against depending on the punctuation marks to tell you when to pause.

If you try to phrase Bible passages according to punctuation, you will find yourself rather perplexed, because different copies or editions of the King James Version itself vary in the punctuation of the same verses. This fact alone should prove that you not only need not but cannot depend on punctuation for phrasing.

Don't phrase **because** of punctuation. You don't look to the punctuation for your phrasing; you look to the punctuation for the **meaning**; then you look to the meaning for the phrasing. Suppose you had to read a sentence like this: " In writing of Robert Louis Stevenson, the essayist, Christopher Morley is warmly enthusiastic." If you relied on punctuation for your phrasing, you would pause after *Stevenson* and *essayist,* as these are followed by commas. And your meaning might be obscure, because your hearers might not be able to tell whether *the essayist* referred to *Stevenson* or *Morley,* since Stevenson wrote essays and so does Morley. So, phrasing according to punctuation here leads to ambiguity. But go to your punctuation for meaning. It shows you that *the essayist* cannot mean Morley, since there is no comma after *Morley.* That is, if *the essayist* referred to Morley, Morley would be

*Reprinted from *Skeptical Essays* by Bertrand Russell, by permission of W. W. Norton and Company, Inc. Copyrighted 1928 by Bertrand Russell.

in apposition with *the essayist* and would have to be set off by commas; if Morley were set off by commas and were in apposition with *the essayist,* then *the essayist* would be the subject of *is warmly enthusiastic.* Since there is no comma after *Morley,* we know that it is not in apposition with *the essayist* and that, therefore, *the essayist* is in apposition with *Stevenson.* Therefore, we make only a very slight pause after *Stevenson* and make a long pause after *essayist.* Thus, we have phrased because of the meaning, not because of the punctuation, although we had to look at the punctuation to find out the meaning.

Don't phrase because of punctuation. You don't look to the punctuation for your phrasing; you look to the punctuation for meaning; then you look to the meaning for the phrasing.

Frequently the meaning will call for a pause where there is no comma or will call for no pause where there is a comma. If there were no more to the science and the art of phrasing than merely pausing for each punctuation mark and nowhere else, there would be little point in all the studying, both with teachers and of books, that public speakers and actors do, or in their intensive practicing of their exercises, lines, and selections. It would be a cut-and-dried, automatic, mechanical process, and every person who could recognize comma, colon, semicolon, period, question mark, and exclamation point would be an effective reader.

Most readers find it is necessary to mark the places where they are going to pause or emphasize. The general habit is to indicate a pause by a comma. This is done, of course, because of the general misconception that the proper place to pause is at a comma. If you are one of those that mark pauses with commas please break the habit now. This is important. It is a very bad idea to associate the thought of a comma with the thought of a pause, because you are then likely to think of the comma as the **cause** of the pause. Use almost any other marking you like. A good idea is to use a vertical line between the words (|) for a short pause and a double line (||) for a longer pause. When you want to indicate that you are not to pause at all, you can use a slur above or below the words that are to be connected without pause.

Third, sometimes a very long sentence will have no internal punctuation at all. It would be very hard for you to breathe and for the listeners to follow your meaning if you never paused until reaching the period.

Here are some of the places (many of which overlap) in which you may pause. At first such a manner of phrasing may seem arbitrary or mechanical to you. But remember that you do not always have to pause at each possible pausing place.

1. *After the subject.*

   The subject of a sentence is very important, because it is, by definition, the thing that you are talking about. You are introducing it to your listeners, and in introductions it is always a good idea to pause after the names of the persons you are introducing: Mrs. Lowell—Mrs. Cabot.

   You may pause after the noun or pronoun which is the subject itself:

   a. That lovely, symmetrical pine tree | is only five years old.

   Or you may pause after the complete subject (with all its modifiers) :

   b. The lovely, symmetrical pine tree growing in our next-door neighbor's yard | is only five years old.

   c. The book that you want | is out of print.

   Sometimes a reader or speaker pauses after the subject even though it consists of only one word. This is done when you wish to focus attention on the subject or make your statement unusually impressive:

   d. I | am a free American.

   e. This | is the Dixie Broadcasting System.

   Perhaps this idea of pausing after the subject seems mechanical and artificial. Evidence that this is a natural place to pause is the fact that many writers erroneously use a comma after the subject, especially if it is a rather long subject. They do this because they are accustomed to sprinkling commas wherever they pause when talking. And remember that your goal in reading is to sound as if you were just talking.

2. *Before the verb.*
Frequently, pausing after the subject means pausing before the verb, as in sentences a. through e. given above. But this is not always true:

    f. The debater argued that such a policy | always, invariably, and inevitably ends in ruin.

3. *After the verb.*

    g. I really believe | every word he has said.

    h. Please indicate | first, second, and third choices.

    i. Today's newspapers have announced | that tomorrow will be a holiday.

4. *Before the direct object.*
This is frequently the same as pausing after the verb, as in sentences g., h., and i. However, there are many times when this is not true:

    j. I really believe literally | every word he has said.

    k. Please indicate clearly | first, second, and third choices.

    l. Would you mind telling me | why you spoke that way?

    m. He has made for himself | a very original and useful career.

5. *Before the predicate noun (also called predicate nominative, subject complement, etc.), predicate adjective, and similar constructions.*

Some of the following examples entail pausing immediately after the verb but some do not:

    n. Next month he will become | the President of our country.

    o. She looks every inch | a duchess.

6. *Before and after a prepositional phrase.*

    p. In his heart | he knew that it would never come to pass.

    q. He knew | in his heart | that it would never come to pass.

r. It will never come to pass, and he knows it | in his heart.

There are numerous other constructions before or after which it is natural to pause but the six just discussed are the simplest on which to begin your practice.

Some of the material about phrasing set forth above (notably, the discussion of the definition and the functions of the pause) is similar to what can be found in numerous books on the subject; but I believe that most of what follows will be particularly helpful, because I have never found anything just like it in any book on the subject, although it seems obviously logical.

TESTS FOR CHANGING A READING

When you decide that logic requires a change from the usual phrasing or emphasis of a passage, you may be pleased with the new way, but if the changes are really drastic it is a good idea to put them to three tests. (1) Does it clarify something usually not understood, or give new meaning?

If it passes this test, you must still ask: (2) Is the clarification important enough to justify your listener's missing the next few sentences while they mull over the surprising new reading?

If it passes this second point, now comes the acid test: (3) Will they get it?

If you've gone through a long, devious train of reasoning that your hearers won't know how to follow, you will only puzzle and perhaps irritate them. If you persist in such reading you will weary them and lose them. You are not reading to startle or to impress with your erudition or originality. You are reading to enlighten and give pleasure. So avoid far-out readings, enticing though they may be.

Some have said to me: "I know these changes in phrasing and emphasis are unusual and surprising, but, now that I've seen the new, sound meaning, I can't go back to the old way." If you are reasonably sure that your audience will grasp what your reading conveys, this may be a good policy to pursue.

V

PHRASING OF SPECIAL CONSTRUCTIONS

RESTRICTIVE AND NONRESTRICTIVE MODIFIERS

It is surprising how much meaning can be brought out by such a simple thing as the correct phrasing of restrictive and nonrestrictive modifiers. Also, it is surprising how many experienced readers fail to read them correctly. It is true that listeners can often piece out the meaning for themselves but they should not be required to do so. The recipients of letters usually manage to decipher poor hand-writing but it is much kinder to write legibly and spare them the trouble. Also, while the hearer is busy puzzling about what has just been read, he fails to hear what follows.

In order to read restrictive and nonrestrictive modifiers correctly, it is necessary, of course, to recall just what they are. (Some grammars call them limiting and nonlimiting clauses or phrases. Others call them defining and nondefining, essential and nonessential.)

A restrictive modifier is one that restricts, confines, or limits the thing or person to one particular thing or person. If a modifier is restrictive, it is necessary to the sense of the sentence, so that it cannot be left out without clouding or ruining the meaning.

In the sentence, " My mother, who now lives in Spokane, is coming to visit me," *who now lives in Spokane* is a nonrestrictive modifier of *mother*. It does not restrict *My mother* to one particular person, as *My mother* does not need to be restricted, since obviously the speaker has only one mother. You may leave out *who now lives in Spokane* without completely changing the meaning or even leaving it in doubt. The gist of the sentence is " My mother is coming to visit me." The fact that she now lives in Spokane is merely thrown in as less vital information.

79

A nonrestrictive modifier merely gives some additional information about the person or thing that is being spoken of. It does not point out one particular person or thing and may be left out without clouding or ruining the meaning.

In the sentence. " The fraternity brother that we just elected president is my room-mate," *that we just elected president* is a restrictive modifier of *brother,* singling out from all the other fraternity brothers the one and only fraternity brother that " we just elected president." Since a person has only one mother, no restrictive modifier is needed; but one has many fraternity brothers (unless one belongs to a very exclusive fraternity, indeed, with only two members!) and, therefore, a restrictive modifier is needed to point out the very one that " we just elected president." Leaving out this restrictive modifier obscures the meaning of the sentence: " The fraternity brother is my room-mate " leaves one wondering " Which fraternity brother? "

In such a sentence as " Every citizen that fails to vote is sadly neglecting his duty," leaving out the restrictive modifier *that fails to vote* not only obscures the meaning but completely changes it, leaving a statement that is absolutely untrue. " Every citizen is sadly neglecting his duty " is obviously false.

Notice that nonrestrictive modifiers should always be set off by commas. Restrictive modifiers should never be set off by commas, because they are too closely connected, too vital, to the meaning of the word they modify to be separated from it by even a comma.

In reading a sentence containing a restrictive modifier, almost never pause before the restrictive modifier, as it is too closely connected with the word it modifies to be separated from it by even a very slight pause, except under unusual circumstances, which will be discussed later.

In reading a sentence containing a nonrestrictive modifier, almost always pause before the nonrestrictive modifier or you will give the impression that it is a restrictive modifier. If you read " My mother, who now lives in Spokane, is coming to visit me " without pausing before *who now lives in Spokane,* you give the senseless impression that the person has several mothers but is speaking of the particular one that now lives in Spokane.

The sentences would probably be phrased as follows:

1. My mother, | who now lives in Spokane, | is coming to visit me.
2. The fraternity brother that we just elected president | is my room-mate.
3. Every citizen that fails to vote | is sadly neglecting his duty.

But, you say, this way of phrasing amounts to nothing more than pausing for a comma and not pausing where there is no comma. There is far more to it than that. The fact that in these sentences the pauses fall at the commas, in some cases, is merely a coincidence. THE COMMA IS NOT THE CAUSE OF THE PAUSE. THE PAUSE IS NOT THE EFFECT OF THE COMMA. THE COMMA AND THE PAUSE ARE BOTH THE EFFECTS OF THE SENSE, which here demands a separation between *mother* and *who now lives in Spokane,* because *who now lives in Spokane* is not needed to identify *mother.*

In the second sentence the sense forbids the use of a pause between *brother* and *that we just elected president,* because *that we just elected president* is vitally needed to designate which brother is meant.

In the third sentence the sense forbids the use of a pause between *citizen* and *that fails to vote,* because *that fails to vote* is vitally needed to designate which citizen is meant.

Notice that you pause after *Spokane, president,* and *vote.* One of these pauses falls at a comma but the other two do not; this shows that the presence or absence of a comma does not affect the phrasing. These three pauses, too, are made because the sense dictates them. They are made after the complete subjects. It would be possible to read the sentences without these three pauses, but reading them with the pauses does make the thought easier to follow, besides giving the reader a logical place to breathe.

The modifier may be a clause (a group of related words containing a subject and a predicate), as in the examples already discussed, or it may be just a phrase (a group of related words not containing a subject and a predicate), as in the following sentences:

4. The man in the moon came down too soon.
5. His wife, next to the piano, is a well-known columnist.

In the moon is a restrictive modifier, a phrase describing *man,* distinguishing the man in the moon from all other men. But *next to the piano* is a phrase modifying *wife* nonrestrictively. It is thrown in merely to tell something extra about *His wife,* to locate her in the room but not to single her out from all other wives, since he is assumed to have only one wife.

One way to test whether a modifier is restrictive or nonrestrictive is to read the sentence without it to see whether it leaves you with a satisfied feeling or with a question in your mind. If we should omit the modifiers we have considered in sentences 1 and 5, our listeners would feel perfectly satisfied with the information that somebody's mother is coming for a visit and that somebody's wife is a well-known columnist. But when we leave them out of sentences 2 and 4, they feel like asking, " Which fraternity brother? " and " What man? " If we should leave out *that fails to vote* in sentence 3 our listeners would find that the rest of the sentence is a misstatement of fact.

Remember, too, that you cannot always depend on a writer's punctuation. The following sentence, only slightly altered, is quoted from a reputable text on American history, just as it was punctuated there: After being shot, Lincoln was taken to a room across the street from the theater where he later died.

As it stands, with no comma after *theater, where he later died* looks like a restrictive modifier of *theater.* A reader depending on commas for his cues to phrase would pause after *shot* (which is a logical place to pause) but would not pause after *theater* and would thus give the impression that Lincoln died in the theater! Of course, his listeners could revise his reading mentally and figure out the meaning, but, by the time they stopped to do this, they would have missed the next phrase or sentence. The listeners should not have to do the reader's work for him!

Browning incorrectly uses commas to separate restrictive modifiers from their antecedents in his poem sometimes called *A Tale:*

" Never more apart you found
Her, he throned, from him, she crowned."

Probably Browning inserted the incorrect commas between *her* and *he* and between *him* and *she* because the rhythm wouldn't allow the relative pronouns *that* or *whom* to be expressed. But read it with no pause at all between *her* and *he* or between *him* and *she*, since it means: Never more apart you found her that he throned from him that she crowned.

" ' Do you reside in Barchester, Dr. Grantley?' asked the lady with her sweetest smile." This sentence from Trollope's *Barchester Towers* should have a comma after *lady*, since *with her sweetest smile* modifies not *lady* but *asked.* Without the comma, it looks like a restrictive modifier of *lady*. So, if you depend on punctuation for your phrasing, you will make no pause after *lady* and you will indicate, not that she asked with her sweetest smile but that it was the lady with her sweetest smile. Whose sweetest smile?

There is an exception to the statement that you should never pause before a restrictive modifier. Sometimes a word and its restrictive modifier are separated. In this case, of course, it is usually better to pause slightly before the restrictive modifier. Otherwise, you would attach the restrictive modifier to some word it did not modify.

The days come no more that brought sorrow and destruction.

Here *days* is the antecedent and *that brought sorrow and destruction* is its restrictive modifier, separated from it by *come no more.* But in this case you may pause or not before *that brought sorrow and destruction,* as there is no danger of making it sound as if it modifies *more.*

The character in the book that I like best is the White Knight.

The antecedent is *character* and its restrictive modifier is *that I like best,* separated from it by *in the book*. It is better here to pause before *that I like best,* or the reader might for a moment think that it modified *book.* The sentence, which is awkwardly worded, refers not to " the book that I like best " but to " The character that I like best."

> " Meantime, worse fates than a lover's fate,
> Who daily may ride and pass and look
> Where his lady watches behind the gate! "

Arranged in prose form, this passage from Browning's *The Statue and the Bust* would read something like this: ". . . worse fates than the fate of a lover who daily may ride . . ." *Who* introduces a restrictive modifier of *lover*. In the poetic version the possessive case is expressed by *lover's,* instead of by *of a lover*. Therefore, the *who* clause is separated from its antecedent, which it would normally be next to and from which it would not be separated by a pause. This is a place where you may pause or not before the restrictive modifier. Since it is a restrictive modifier, it might be well to keep it as close as possible to *lover's* because there is little danger that the reader would think that it modified *fate*. In other words, the reader wouldn't be likely to think that you were reading about a fate who daily might ride, etc.

Sometimes the relative word (who, whom, which, that) is not expressed, especially in informal and colloquial writing, as " This is the man I married," instead of " This is the man that I married." (*That I married* is the restrictive modifier of *man*.)

A proof that there should be no pause at all between an antecedent and its restrictive modifier is found in sentences like these:

> That which you say, I am certain, is false.
> He who follows his conscience is usually safe.

That and *which* are so closely related that they can easily be fused into one word, *what*. *He* and *who,* similarly, can be replaced by a single word, *whoever*.

> What you say, I am certain, is false.
> Whoever follows his conscience is safe.

Sometimes, especially in poetry, the antecedent is not expressed, as in the following sentence:

Who walks in prayer along this path feels not the roughness of the way.

Normally it would read, He who walks in prayer along this path feels not the roughness of the way. With a construction like this, be careful not to stress the *who,* or you will sound as if you are asking a question: Who walks in prayer? Practice reading the sentence with the *He* expressed and you will see that you naturally stress *He, walks,* and *prayer,* and subdue *who.* This gives the key to the natural way to read it when the *He* is omitted: Jump rapidly over *who,* giving it no stress.

" In 1858 Puccini was born in Lucca." Failure to make a short pause after *born* might cause someone who is really paying attention to you to think of the nonsensical question, " If he was born in 1858 in Lucca, when was he born in Rome or Naples? "

Two Things Logically Connected with a Third

Frequently in writing, and once in a while in just talking, we use a construction something like this: a) Charles went into and out of the room. Or: b) They have frequently tested and thoroughly proved the secretary's integrity. Or: c) She is a very considerate, and, what's more, a very delightful companion for a long trip.

This construction might be called " two things grammatically connected with a third." In a) we have the two prepositions *into* and *out of* grammatically connected with *the room.* In other words, *room* is the object of *into* and also it is the object of *out of.* (The sentence might have been worded: He went into the room and out of the room.) This construction is not heard very often in spontaneous conversation, in which we usually use short sentences with uncomplicated constructions. But a simple sentence like a) could very easily be used in conversation. If you will listen carefully to the way people naturally phrase such a construction when just talking, you will find that they invariably phrase them logically, although without having to stop to consider, just as they don't have to stop to reason about whether they're going to use a rising or a falling inflection when they ask a spontaneous question.

The way we would naturally speak this sentence would be to pause after *into* and after *out of;* or, we might pause after *out of* and not pause after *into.* But we would not pause after *into* unless we also paused after *out of.* Why? Because that would make it sound as if the room were the object of *out of* but not of *into*. It would make the meaning, *out of the room*, clear, but it would leave *into* just hanging. Into what?

So the main point is to be sure to pause before *the room*, to make it clear that *the room* does not belong to *out of* exclusively. If you read the sentence with a pause after *into* and no pause after *out of*, *into* is already separated from its object, *the room*, by several words; then you must separate *out of*, also, from their common object, *the room*, or it will appropriate the object for itself and leave nothing to be the object of *into*.

There is still another way to phrase this construction logically and naturally; without a pause after either *into* or *out of*. So you have a choice of three logical ways to phrase this construction:

1. Pause after the two things grammatically connected with the third. Charles went into | and out of | the room.
2. Do not pause after either of the two things grammatically connected with the third. Charles went into and out of the room.
3. Pause only before the third thing, with which the first two are connected. Charles went into and out of | the room.

There is one way (at least) to read it illogically and unnaturally; Charles went into | and out of the room. (This puts a pause after the first thing and no pause before the third thing.)

The same thing applies even if the sentence has much more to it: Charles went into and then, apparently in great alarm, ran hastily out of the room. Here there is more danger that someone might read it with a pause after *into* and no pause after *out of*, because the construction is more complicated. This is the type of sentence you would be more likely to see written than to hear spoken. And when you are reading aloud a long sentence with this construction you have to trust to logical thinking and analysis rather than to your ear. But you may be surprised at how quickly you can train yourself to look ahead and see this construction. And, once you have trained yourself to recognize it and read it the reasonable way, it will sound very unpleasant to you when you hear someone read it the other way. And don't try to persuade yourself that at least some of your hearers won't appreciate the right way and be jarred by the wrong.

Once in a great while, especially when the sentence is long and involved, the writer will use commas; but don't depend on them, as frequently they will be incorrectly used. Correctly, there could be a comma after each of the prepositions: Charles walked into, and out of, the room. Or, correctly, there could be no comma after either of the prepositions: Charles walked into and out of the room. It would be incorrect to use the first comma without the other: Charles walked into, and out of the room. So this is one more instance of the danger of depending on commas for your phrasing.

Besides phrasing this construction according to the preceding instruction, we sometimes naturally place a little emphasis on the third thing, too.

WHEN YOU READ A SENTENCE CONTAINING TWO THINGS GRAMMATICALLY CONNECTED WITH A THIRD (OR THREE WITH A FOURTH, OR FOUR WITH A FIFTH, ETC.), PAUSE AFTER EACH OF THE TWO THINGS GRAMMATICALLY CONNECTED WITH THE THIRD; OR, AT LEAST, PAUSE BEFORE THE THIRD. DO NOT PAUSE AFTER THE FIRST UNLESS YOU PAUSE AFTER THE SECOND.

This construction does not always consist of two prepositions with the same object. Sometimes you will find two verbs with the same object, as in b) in the first paragraph of this section. Here *tested* and *proved* are the two things grammatically connected with the third, *the secretary's integrity.* Or you will find two adjectives modifying the same noun, as in c) in the first paragraph. Here you have *considerate* and *delightful,* two things grammatically connected with a third, *companion.*

Again, you may find a more complicated construction, such as: The bather surveyed and then dived into the water. Here *the water* is the third thing, connected with (object of) the verb *surveyed* (first thing) and also object of the preposition *into* (third thing). Many readers would thoughtlessly just stop after the two verbs.

surveyed and *dived:* The bather surveyed | and then dived | into the water. But this would make it sound as if *into the water* were connected with both *surveyed* and *dived.* It would mean: The bather surveyed into the water and dived into the water.

Of course, you may say, the reader could figure out the sense, anyway. Yes, but that is not his function. Also, there are certain sentences containing this construction which are too ambiguous to leave to the listener to straighten out for himself. Sometimes they are too complicated for the reader to figure out at sight: Five hundred Japanese soldiers were killed or ordered to commit suicide by their officers. If you phrase a sentence like this one way it means one thing; if another, it means something entirely different. If you make a long pause after *killed* and none at all after *suicide,* you clearly imply that *ordered to commit suicide* goes with *by their officers* but that *were killed* does not; that is, they were killed by the enemy or their officers ordered them to commit suicide. If you think it means that their officers either killed them or ordered them to commit suicide, you have your choice of two ways to phrase it: You may pause after both *killed* and *suicide,* or you may pause after *suicide* only. But when you run across a sentence with such an easily misunderstood meaning, you must underscore your phrasing. When you pause, pause a long time and unmistakably. When you conclude that there should be no pause, rush along and make sure that your hearers know that you are not pausing.

Sometimes a sentence is so ambiguous that you can't read it intelligently until you have done some research on it: " And the fourth kingdom shall be as strong as iron: forasmuch as iron breaketh in pieces and subdueth all things: and as iron that breaketh all these, shall it break in pieces and bruise " (Daniel 2:40). Without either consulting some other Bible translations or going back to the original language, it is almost impossible to discover the meaning here. Obviously it means that iron subdues all things; but does it mean that iron breaks all things in pieces or that iron merely breaks in pieces itself? Dr. Moffatt's translation gives this as: " for, as iron breaks everything to bits and beats it down." * Therefore, we know that *all*

---

*From *The Bible: A New Translation,* by James Moffatt. Copyrighted 1935 by Harper & Brothers. Used by permission.

things is the object of *breaketh in pieces* as well as the object of *subdueth*. In order to show this, you should make a long and unmistakable pause before *all things* (the third thing, with which the first two, *breaketh in pieces* and *subdueth* are connected).

Some sentences are so ambiguous that it is almost impossible to figure out what they actually mean and where the pauses should come, like: He has often tested and has now finally determined the value of that invention. Does the second pause fall after *determined* or after *of? The value* is the object of *determined,* of course, but what is the object of *tested?* Does it mean he tested that invention or he tested the value of that invention? It could be either.

Suppose you are reading a sentence like this: We often correspond with and see them. The meaning is quite clear: We correspond with them and see them. *Them* is the third thing, the object of the first two things, *correspond with* and *see*. But, since the third thing is only a very small pronoun, it would sound peculiar and stilted to pause before *them;* so make no pause at all after either *with* or *see*. Be especially careful that you do not put a pause after *with* with no pause after *see*. In short, there are at least three ways in which this sentence may be phrased: 1) Illogically: We correspond with | and see them. 2) Logically but stiltedly: We correspond with | and see | them. 3) Logically and naturally: We correspond with and see them. (No pause at all.)

Naturally the same thing would apply if the sentence read: We often see and correspond with them. (Don't pause after either *see* or *with* and be especially careful not to pause after *see* with no pause after *with*.) But, if the little pronoun *them* were changed to a longer expression, then the usual way of phrasing this construction could be followed without a stilted effect: We often correspond with and see | our good friends in Colorado. A pause after *see* and no pause after *with* probably would be the most effective way to phrase it now, unless you were reading in a very large auditorium. In that case you might well pause after *with* and after *see*.

Athough such constructions can be very puzzling, logical reasoning usually uncovers the meaning. But sometimes it seems easier just to feed out words for our listeners than to apply logical thinking. And even after the meaning is clear to the reader, he still cannot give it to his hearers unless he knows the principles of phrasing, emphasis, and inflection.

It is in sentences like " The bather surveyed and then dived into the water," that most mistakes are made, because the reader doesn't stop to figure out where the breaks really occur.

Many readers always hit the prepositions very hard in a sentence like this: The secondary condition is related to and dependent upon the former. The breaks occur after *to* and *upon,* two prepositions with the same object, *the former.* So you may pause after each preposition, at least taking care to pause before *the former.* But if you always stress the prepositions in such constructions, it tends to become a mannerism. Once in a while stress the preceding verbs or adjectives instead (*related* and *dependent*).

Don't ever fall into the habit of reading the same construction the same way every time if there is any other reasonable way to read it. Try to give your reading variety as well as logic and naturalness.

Occasionally you will find this construction in reverse, that is, the " third " thing will precede the two things which are both connected with it. " Whether is easier, to say, Thy sins be forgiven thee: or to say, Rise up and walk? " (Luke 5:23.) There can be no doubt of the way to phrase this verse, and yet it is phrased wrong distressingly often. It does not give a choice of two things to say: " Thy sins be forgiven thee " or " Rise up and walk." It gives a choice of two alternatives: 1) to say, " Thy sins be forgiven thee," or 2) to say, " Rise up and walk." So, of course, you should pause before each *to say,* and, to make the meaning doubly clear, you might take care not to pause after either *to say.*

If you remember how to diagram a sentence you will find diagramming a great help for seeing the construction and meaning of sentences like these.

CONNECTING WORD FOLLOWED BY A PARENTHETICAL EXPRESSION SET OFF BY COMMAS

Most radio stations require that all material used be written out and read instead of being spoken spontaneously. Therefore, there is a premium on the ability to read from the printed page and make it sound like spur-of-the-moment talking. One way that amateur—

and many professional—readers give away the fact that they are reading from a printed page is their manner of reading a sentence that contains a connecting word followed by a parenthetical expression set off by commas. This description sounds a little formidable but it is easy to recognize this construction:

We feel that, in the event of new developments, she should be notified.

That is the connecting word, followed by the parenthetical expression, *in the event of new developments,* set off by commas.

Because most people feel obligated to pause before a comma as before a red light, they pause after *that* and after *developments.* Because most untrained line-readers seem unable to pause without emphasizing or holding the word immediately preceding the pause, they stress both *that* and *developments.* It is all right to stress *developments,* because it conveys an important idea (although, perhaps, *new* is more important) but to stress *that* produces a very unnatural reading. It is unnatural, literally, because that is not the way you would say it naturally in conversation. And the reason you would not stress *that* when spontaneously talking is that *that* has little or no meaning, being merely a connecting word. You could even leave it out completely.

So, to read this sentence stressing—or holding—*that* and pausing before *in,* immediately betrays the fact that you are reading aloud and not just talking. Train yourself to listen for this type of sentence and you will find that the spontaneous speaker subdues the connecting word and makes no pause before the word that follows it, set off from the connecting word by a comma. This indicates that, in the sample sentence above, you should subdue the *that* so that it becomes merely *th't* (not *thut*), and then you should make no pause between *that* and *in,* even though there is a comma between them. (Of course, sentences of this type are a little too studied to be heard in conversation as often as simpler constructions but you will hear them often enough to agree that they should be phrased as suggested here.)

WHEN READING A SENTENCE CONTAINING A CONNECTING WORD, ESPECIALLY A RELATIVE, FOLLOWED BY A PARENTHETICAL EXPRESSION SET OFF BY COMMAS, SUBDUE THE CONNECTING WORD AND DO NOT PAUSE AFTER IT.

Here is proof that people actually phrase such constructions this way. Many, probably most, persons punctuate their writing with little thought for rules of grammar and punctuation. They merely pepper their sentences with commas wherever they would pause when speaking, sometimes using a comma where a semicolon is required, sometimes using one where no punctuation at all is needed. Thus, one of the most common mistakes in punctuation, made even by scholarly writers, is leaving out the first comma in such a construction but putting in the second. Punctuated in this incorrect but usual manner, the sentence would read:

We feel that in the event of new developments, she should be notified.

Why do people make this particular mistake in punctuation? Because they are using commas promiscuously **wherever they pause in speaking,** instead of where the rules of grammar call for commas. It is almost safe to say that you will never find this type of sentence incorrectly punctuated with the first comma used and the second omitted. Why? Because nobody phrases this type of construction that way when using it in conversation. In other words, you are almost certain never to find a sentence incorrectly punctuated like this:

We feel that, in the event of new developments she should be notified.

There are two ways of punctuating this sentence correctly:

We feel that, in the event of new developments, she should be notified.
We feel that in the event of new developments she should be notified.

Whichever way it is punctuated, the reader should never pause after *that* (because the speaker wouldn't). Also, the speaker, if in a great hurry, might not pause after *developments;* but the oral reader, even if he has enough breath to read the whole thing without a pause, should not read such a long sentence without phrasing, and almost the only logical place to pause is after *developments.* Even in a short sentence it is usually advisable to pause after the last word of the parenthetical expression.

A further proof of the soundness of this principle is this: In conversation we almost never hear anyone pause after the connecting word, whether it is followed by a parenthetical expression or followed directly by the grammatical group it introduces.

We feel that she should be notified.

Nobody uttering this sentence spontaneously would think of pausing between the connecting word, *that,* and the group it introduces, *she should be notified.* It is safe to follow the policy, therefore, of never pausing between a connecting word and the parenthetical expression unless it is one of those rare sentences where you might pause between the connecting word and the group it introduces, even if there were no parenthetical expression separating them. You will soon develop a feeling for the natural and therefore correct phrasing of this construction; but, until you do, it will be well to test each one by reading it without the parenthetical expression to see whether you might possibly pause after the connecting word, anyway. You will seldom find a sentence in which you have any justification for pausing after the connecting word.

Remember that it sounds just as unnatural to emphasize the connecting word or to prolong it as it does to pause after it.

Sometimes it is easier (on the speaker's breathing) and clearer to the listener to pause before the connecting word, still taking care not to emphasize it or pause after it. This usually is advisable when there is a long clause before the connecting word.

Undoubtedly every one of them will be delighted to receive the information that, almost without exception, their candidates were elected.

Unless the reader pauses before *that,* he might try to go all the way through *exception* without a pause.

Some of the connecting words (conjunctions and relative pronouns) that you may look for are: *that, if, when, while, where, who, which, because, as, since, for, although, lest, inasmuch as.*

Be careful about reading this construction in a very familiar passage, like the first sentence of the Declaration of Independence. In passages like these, which we have been accustomed from childhood to hear chanted in a time-honored way, usually meaningless, it is surprising how much freshness and undiscovered meaning can be drawn out by simply reading them according to the suggestions you are studying.

" When, in the Course of human events, it becomes necessary for one people . . ."

Here, **pausing** after the connecting word *When* is not the general error; it is **stressing** the connecting word *When.* Most people, from kindergarteners up, hit the first word very hard. Probably the reason this meaningless stress was made in the first place is that the first words in the sentence that carry real meaning are *human events,* or, perhaps, *Course,* and, unless the reader or speaker comes down fairly heavily on *When,* he has to limp along to the fourth or the sixth word before finding a place to rest the emphasis. It really should be read with no stress before *Course* and no pause until just before *it.*

At first, *When* in this quotation may not seem like a connecting word. But consider the sentence in its entirety: " When, in the Course of human events, it becomes necessary for one people to dissolve the political bands which have connected them with another, and to assume among the powers of the earth, the separate and equal station to which the Laws of Nature and of Nature's God entitle them, a decent respect to the opinions of mankind requires that they should declare the causes which impel them to the separation."

Now recast it into its normal grammatical form, with the main clause first: A decent respect to the opinions of mankind requires

that they should declare the causes which impel them to the separation, when (in the Course of human events) it becomes necessary
for one people to dissolve the political bands which have connected
them with another. You see that *When* connects the subordinate
clause, *it becomes necessary for one people to dissolve the political
bands,* with the main part, *a decent respect to the opinions of mankind requires that they should declare the causes which impel them
to the separation.*

Occasionally a reader unnaturally emphasizes the connecting
word and pauses after it, even when the parenthetical expression is
not set off by commas, especially when the rhythm would suggest
this emphasis, as in the following stanza from Lewis Carroll's *Jabber-
wocky:*

> "And as in uffish thought he stood,
> The Jabberwock, with eyes of flame,
> Came whiffling through the tulgey wood,
> And burbled as it came! "

As is the connecting word; *in uffish thought,* the parenthetical
expression.

There is a school of thought that insists that poetry should be
stressed according to rhythm and not according to sense, where the
two conflict. There is much to be said for this argument, particularly
in poetry as rhythmical as Lewis Carroll's, where stressing the
rhythm brings out even more fun and more music. In purely lyrical
poetry and especially in philosophical or didactic poetry, however,
probably it is best to stress according to the meaning.

VOCATIVES

Nobody would ever think of saying, " Come in—Louise-and-sit-
down," as it is natural to say, " Come-in-Louise—and sit down."
Likewise, if one were reading the sentence, " Come in, Louise, and
sit down," he would not have to be told not to pause before *Louise.*
He would naturally connect *Louise* with *Come in* and would pause
after *Louise,* if at all. This would be true whether or not he had
ever heard of what is called a vocative. (The first, and accented,
syllable of vocative rhymes with lock; the vocative is the case of

address; it is the name or the title of the person or thing you are speaking to, like *Louise* in the sentence above, or *pretty maiden* in " Tell me, pretty maiden, are there any more at home like you? " or *door* in " Now stay open, door, and don't bang shut again! ")

For some reason, in spontaneous talking we almost always connect the vocative with what precedes and not with what follows. (Many of our ways of spontaneously phrasing and emphasizing can be explained logically but many, like this one, are unexplainable.) Listen to the talk around you and you will see that this is the way people phrase unconsciously when they use vocatives. The habit is so ingrained that almost anyone would automatically use this phrasing in reading aloud the prose sentences quoted above. But when people begin to read poetry they do not always read this construction naturally.

There are several explanations for this. In the first place, the thought of reading poetry causes many persons to be self-conscious at the outset and makes them do things they wouldn't otherwise do. Also, poetry often has a strong rhythm, which causes readers to pause at the ends of lines, regardless of the sense. Readers of hymns are even more inclined to do this, because we are accustomed usually to hearing the words of hymns not only read but sung with strong emphasis on the rhythm, regardless of the meaning. In fact, one reason that the words of hymns are read aloud with a jingly effect is that we are so accustomed to singing them, and in singing we have to pause for the rhythm, whether it fits the meaning or not. Rhythm in singing poetry is more or less inflexible but rhythm in reading it should not be, unless one is interested solely in the musical effect and not in the significance.

Try reading aloud the first stanza of *America*. You are an unusually discerning reader if you made a rather long pause before, and almost no pause after, *'tis of thee*. Because of the rhythm and the rhyme, most people read it just as they sing it, with no pause before *'tis of thee* and a long pause before *sweet land of liberty*. They read it as if My-country-'tis-of-thee were all one word. This phrasing is so habitual that the song is often called *My Country, 'Tis of Thee* instead of *America*. Yet those five words strung together make no sense without the eight that follow to complete the sentence.

You are talking to *My country* or *sweet land of liberty*. Therefore, they are both vocatives; so *sweet land of liberty* would naturally follow *'tis of thee* without a pause. *My country*, however, has nothing preceding it and you could read it naturally either with or without a pause following it. However, since it is almost always followed by *'tis of thee* with no pause at all, it might be a good idea to pause noticeably between *country* and *'tis*.

Perhaps it would make it clearer to make up a sentence with exactly the same construction. Because you have not been reading the following sentence a certain way all your life, you will be more likely to approach it spontaneously; My friend, it is of you, dear, of you I am thinking. The vocatives, *my friend*, and *dear*, correspond to *My country* and *Sweet land of liberty*, respectively; *it is of you* corresponds with *'tis of thee*, and *of you I am thinking* corresponds with *of thee I sing*. Now you may or may not pause after *friend;* you probably will pause after *dear;* but, if you read it as you would talk it, you will certainly not pause before *dear*. And undoubtedly you wouldn't put a pause between *you* and *dear* with no pause at all between *dear* and *of*.

There is exactly the same construction in the last stanza. It is usually read because of the way it has to be sung, as: " Our-fathers'-God-to-Thee,—Author of liberty, to Thee we sing." But it should be: "Our fathers' God,—to Thee, Author of liberty, To Thee we sing."

QUOTATIONS

Don't let anyone persuade you that you are supposed to stop and wait before and after a quotation. You don't have to signal to your hearers that a quotation is coming or has just ended. When reading you should be thinking about the sense, not about the punctuation, as you do not think in terms of punctuation marks when you are just talking. Never lose sight of the fact that you are merely trying to make your listeners think that you are simply talking to them. The last part of Hebrews 13:2 reads: ". . . for thereby some have entertained angels unawares." The last two words are quoted together so often that many have come to think of them as though *unawares* modified *angels*. But it does not; *unawares* modifies *some*. It isn't the angels that were unawares; it's **some** that were unawares. Rearranged into the normal order, it would read: Some, unawares, have entertained angels.

Suppose you should run across a sentence like this: In giving them shelter, you were hosts to " angels unawares." Now don't let the quotation marks trick you; don't stop before *angels,* as though you were announcing: " Quotation marks coming! " Think of the sense and not of the punctuation. You don't mean that some people were hosts to angels that were unawares. You mean that some people, unawares, were hosts to angels. Therefore, do not pause before the two quoted words and then read them as though they were one word. They don't even belong to each other grammatically. If there were no quotation marks there and if you had never heard the quotation, you would naturally read it with no pause between *to* and *angels* (there is almost never a pause between a preposition and its object, anyway; their relationship is so close that even quotation marks cannot separate them) and with a definite pause between *angels* and *unawares.*

FINDING TWO IDEAS INSTEAD OF ONLY ONE

Sometimes you run across a sentence that is usually read in one lump and, therefore, is made to convey just one idea but which really has two or more important ideas which can be brought out if the reader sees them and if he knows how to make them stand out. Genesis 1:27 begins: " So God created man in his own image." Usually the reader is so intent on the idea of " in his own image " that he misses the opportunity of bringing out something important: first, that man was created by God; second, he was created in God's image. These two ideas can be utilized by pausing after *man,* letting the reader grasp that much of the sentence as important in itself, and then going on to add another important thought: *in his own image.*

Usually, if this can be done at all, it is done by stopping after the verb or after the verb and its object. This concentrates attention on the thought in the verb, establishing the verb's idea. Then you can proceed to read its modifiers or its object. Thus, instead of focusing attention upon the sentence as a whole and especially on the last part, you let your listeners receive the idea in the verb and get the good out of it and then add the other idea to it.

Form the habit of analyzing your sentences to see whether they are constructed in this way. But don't make a mannerism of reading them like this. Use this trick of phrasing only when two ideas are really worth bringing out separately or it will lose its effect and your reading will become monotonous.

"And straightway his ears were opened, and the string of his tongue was loosed, and he spake plain" (Mark 7:35). A great deal of the wonderful force of this verse is often lost because readers don't think of pausing after *spake*. The last four words usually are read with no pause. Saying that he spake-plain is not so impressive as emphasizing *spake* and then making a rather long pause after it. This gives the hearer time to ponder the fact that he spake at all, which was wonderful. Then adding the word *plain,* after a pause, adds another wonder, the fact that he not only spake but also spake plain. Although he may never have heard a word spoken, he was able to speak, and to speak distinctly, without having to learn to use his speech mechanism or to build up a vocabulary. All this is implied in the well-thought-out pause after *spake*.

"And they did all eat, and were filled: and they took up of the broken meat that was left seven baskets full" (Matthew 15:37). This construction is similar. Here, too, much of the impressiveness is neglected by not pausing before the last word. Often it is read with no pause at all between *baskets* and *full,* as though it were seven basketfuls. But there is a difference between a basketful and a basket full or a full basket. The point here is that there was enough left over to fill seven baskets, and that the baskets were full. This idea is given out by pausing after *baskets* and stressing *full*.

"And the Lord went before them by day in a pillar of a cloud, to lead them in the way; and by night in a pillar of fire" (Exodus 13:21). If you pause after the first *them* long enough to focus attention on the idea of the Lord's going before them, you give your hearers one helpful idea to think about. Then you add another: the manner in which the Lord went before them by day and the manner by night. As this is frequently read, with no pause after the first *them,* the reader is rushing on to tell about the cloud and the fire and gives the listener no time to ponder the first helpful idea. The listener might just as well be allowed to enjoy two helpful thoughts instead of one, since they are both undeniably present in the text. Of course, though, there is nothing wrong or misleading about reading it the usual way; so here again the reader can make his choice of more than one " correct " reading.

Ephesians 4:24 also provides a legitimate place to emphasize two thoughts instead of hurrying from the first to place most of the stress on the second. You can do this by pausing decidedly after *created.* You may or may not like this reading. " And that ye put on the new man, which after God is created in righteousness and true holiness."

Sometimes you will find passages where giving two ideas is not merely a matter of choice, passages where two ideas ought to be given instead of just one or the meaning will be changed. In Genesis 4:4 there is usually no pause made after *brought.* This implies an illogical meaning. " And Abel, he also brought of the firstlings of his flock and of the fat thereof." If you say without pause that " Abel also brought of the firstlings of his flock," you imply that Cain, too, had " brought of the firstlings of his flock." But the *also* goes with *brought* only, not with the whole thing. Therefore, you need to make a separation after *brought.* What Abel also did was simply to bring. He did not " also bring of the firstlings of his flock." So a definite pause after *brought,* together with a falling inflection, establishes the idea. Then you add the very important idea that what he brought was " of the firstlings of his flock."

Overuse of this idea can result in something much worse than merely an annoying mannerism. It can produce officious personal interpretation, or, more accurately stated, misinterpretation. Both Moffatt's translation and the Greek text show that it would be definitely wrong to stop after *me* in the second verse of Romans 8: " For the law of the Spirit of life in Christ Jesus hath made me free from the law of sin and death." Don't attempt to establish the idea that the law has made me (created me) and then add a second idea, that it has not only created me but created me free. The verb is not *to make;* it is *to make free* or *to free.* So the only right way to read this is the usual way of reading *made me free* with no pause between *me* and *free*.

WHAT DOES IT MODIFY OR BELONG WITH?

Certain adverbs, especially the small word *not*, go a long way toward spoiling the reading of a good many passages read by persons who do not analyze the sentences carefully enough to see what they really mean and, almost as important, what they do not mean. The test is to see whether the adverb modifies what precedes it or what follows. Hearing it read in connection with the wrong word is very disconcerting to those listeners who know the right way from the wrong. And do not underestimate the intelligence of your audience. Intelligent listeners are becoming more and more numerous, as are intelligent readers.

" There is therefore now no condemnation to them which are in Christ Jesus, who walk not after the flesh, but after the Spirit " (Romans 8:1). There are two logical ways to read the last ten words and one illogical way. Many readers, through failing to arrive at the real meaning for themselves, unconsciously give out the illogical reading: they pause slightly after *not* and do not pause after *walk*. This makes *not* modify *walk*. But it isn't saying that they walk not; it's saying that they walk " not after the flesh but after the Spirit." Therefore, to make it perfectly clear, you should pause slightly before *not* and make no pause at all after *not*. Don't pause too long before *not;* don't be ostentatious about knowing where to pause. There is only one other way to phrase it without spoiling the sense: don't pause either before or after *not*. This reading doesn't bring out the real sense especially well but at least it doesn't give the wrong sense.

In Ephesians 4:17 we read: " This I say therefore, and testify in the Lord, that ye henceforth walk not as other Gentiles walk, in the vanity of their mind." Here *not* modifies the *walk* that precedes it; it does not go with *as other Gentiles* walk. In order to go with what follows it, it always has to mean " not this but that "—" not so-and-so but such-and-such." Here it would have to be " not as the Gentiles walk but as somebody else walks." But, if you follow this long sentence to its end at the close of verse 19, you will see that the way the Gentiles walk is not contrasted with the way anybody else walks. It says merely not to walk as they walk. Therefore, you should pause slightly after *not* or else pause neither before nor after *not.* The main thing is to be sure not to pause before *not,* as this leaves your listeners with a question in their minds: Well, not as the Gentiles walk but as who walks?

The adverb *first* in Matthew 13:30 is frequenty read incorrectly: " Gather ye together first the tares, and bind them in bundles to burn them: but gather the wheat into my barn." It doesn't say: Gather first the tares and then the wheat. It says: First gather the tares and then gather the wheat. So you should make no pause before *first* but make a pause after *first.* If you pause before *first,* you raise a question for the listener who is really paying attention to you: first the tares and then the—what?

Of course, there are some sentences you will find which you cannot possibly phrase correctly because they aren't written grammatically, sentences like this: She intended not to invite Kathleen but Evelyn to the party. In this sentence it isn't correct to phrase *not* with *intended* and it isn't correct to phrase it with *invite,* since it doesn't modify either of them. Logically it belongs with *Kathleen* and the sentence should have been written: She intended to invite not Kathleen but Evelyn to the party. In this case you would pause slightly before *not,* if anywhere. Of course, you wouldn't pause after *not,* as this would connect *not* with *invite.*

POETRY AND HYMNS

Many persons are a little more hesitant about reading verse than about reading prose. Sometimes the meaning is not so easy to follow, because of inverted word order, for instance. Therefore, it is frequently advisable to rearrange verse into the normal prose order. See the answer to the thirteenth exercise in the Answer Book for Chapter III. If you are reading poetry which is as complicated as that of Robert Browning, it is almost necessary to rewrite it into the natural, or prose, order; then practice reading it in that form. See which words are emphasized and which are subdued. Then, when you read it again in its verse form, stress and subdue the same words, even though the rhythm may call for different handling.

If you remember how to diagram, it is often very helpful to diagram poetry, even though this may seem a rather cold-blooded way to handle anything so delicate as a poem. Frequently, readers who have thought that they understood a poem or a hymn very well have found that on using the recasting and diagramming methods, there was much meaning there which they had not seen at all. Also, students trying to learn the meaning of a certain poem or hymn have seen its meaning suddenly when they applied these principles.

A mistake to avoid is " jingling." This tendency is due to the pronounced rhythm of some verse; there is a very strong impulse to stop at the end of every line, whether the sense calls for a stop or not. Jingling and most of the other faults of reading verse or hymns are often caused by great familiarity with the material; we have heard it jingled so long that we hardly think of the real meaning. Also, a verse put to music must be phrased according to the stopping-places of the melody; then, when you take the words away from the music and read them aloud, it is very hard not to phrase them according to the musical phrasing, even when it conflicts with the sense.

Often, jingling is a matter of wrong inflection as well as of wrong phrasing or emphasis, as in the following poem by Thomas Moore:

" Believe me, if all those endearing young charms,
    Which I gaze on so fondly today,
Were to change by tomorrow and fleet in my arms,
    Like fairy gifts fading away,
Thou would'st still be adored, as this moment thou art,
    Let thy loveliness fade as it will,
And around the dear ruin each wish of my heart,
    Would entwine itself verdantly still."

You might logically make a very slight pause after *charms* and after *arms,* because of the sense. Or the sense would allow you to omit pauses after *charms* and *arms.* But many people in reading the words aloud would not only pause after *charms* but stop completely, also using a falling inflection as if it were the end of a sentence. Also, they would make no pause after *me.* The cause of such reading is easily found. It is the fact that the first eight words are the title of the song and usually are spoken in one gulp. But just think about the meaning and you will read it in a fresher way: Believe me: if all those endearing young charms were to change by tomorrow and fleet in my arms, thou would'st still be adored.

Sometimes a thought carries not only from one line over and back to the next but from one stanza to the next. If this is the case, do not pause at the end of a stanza any more than you would at the end of a line. Even when you are reading the words from a song book or a hymnal and one stanza ends at the bottom of the right-hand page and the next stanza begins at the top of the following left-hand page, if the thought carries over, don't hesitate a moment between stanzas. Remember: you are always trying to indicate to your hearers an idea rather than the arrangement of words on a page.

This applies also to a few places in the Bible where one verse ends with a comma or with no punctuation at all, since the following verse is a continuation of the sentence begun in the first verse. In such places, phrase the two verses as though they were written with no separation.

Two Ideas in Conjunction

" Though a sinner do evil an hundred times, and his days be prolonged, yet surely I know that it shall be well with them that fear God, which fear before him " (Ecclesiastes 8:12). Surely this verse does not mean: I know it shall be well with them that fear God, though a sinner do evil an hundred times. It does not mean: I know that it shall be well with them that fear God, though a sinner's days be prolonged. Neither condition is significant by itself; that is, the mere fact that a sinner does wrong is not especially disturbing and the mere fact that someone's days are prolonged is not disturbing. It is when the two things happen together that we might be disturbed; when a sinner does evil an hundred times and still his days are prolonged. Therefore, do not separate the two ideas by pausing after *times.* Read it almost as one idea, with no definite pause until after *prolonged.*

RESTRICTIVE AND NONRESTRICTIVE MODIFIERS

Try not pausing before each restrictive modifier. Try pausing before each nonrestrictive modifier. (You can't depend on the punctuation here, because no commas have been used. You must decide whether the modifiers are restrictive or nonrestrictive and then phrase accordingly. It would be a good idea to write in the commas where you decide they should be.)

1. The man that is sitting in the gold chair is going to make a speech.

2. The man sitting in the gold chair is going to make a speech.

3. The man in the gold chair is going to make a speech.

4. Our President who is sitting in the gold chair is going to make a speech.

5. Our President sitting in the gold chair is going to make a speech.

6. Our President in the gold chair is going to make a speech.

7. This is the man we've been looking for!

8. Are you the person that found a wallet?

9. That author whose novels I have enjoyed for years has recently written a book of essays.

10. Are you familiar with Thomas Hardy's poem called *The Man He Killed?*

11. This map which is ten years old has a number of inaccuracies.

12. I am going to call on my twin brother whom I haven't seen for fifteen years.

13. " To him who in the love of Nature holds communion with her visible forms she speaks a various language."—Bryant: *Thanatopsis.*

14. " And she—she watched the square like a book
    Holding one picture and only one
    Which daily to find she undertook."—Browning: *The Statue and the Bust.*

In the following quotations the original punctuation has been used:

15. "For he that cometh to God must believe that he is, and that he is a rewarder of them that diligently seek him" (Hebrews 11:6).

16. "For he looked for a city which hath foundations, whose builder and maker is God" (Hebrews 11:10).

17. "Man that is born of a woman is of few days, and full of trouble" (Job 14:1).

18. "Wherefore I say unto thee, Her sins, which are many, are forgiven; for she loved much" (Luke 7:47).

19. "The Lord will perfect that which concerneth me" (Psalm 138:8).

20. "And the Lord God planted a garden eastward in Eden; and there he put the man whom he had formed" (Genesis 2:8).

21. "Go to now, ye rich men, weep and howl for your miseries that shall come upon you" (James 5:1).

22. "For God, who commanded the light to shine out of darkness, hath shined in our hearts" (II Corinthians 4:6).

23. "And, behold, men brought in a bed a man which was taken with a palsy" (Luke 5:18).

24. "And Jacob called unto his sons, and said, Gather yourselves together, that I may tell you that which shall befall you in the last days" (Genesis 49:1).

25. "Judah, thou art he whom thy brethren shall praise" (Genesis 49:8).

26. "Behold, I will send my messenger, and he shall prepare the way before me: and the Lord, whom ye seek, shall suddenly come to his temple, even the messenger of the covenant, whom ye delight in" (Malachi 3:1).

27. "The way of the wicked is an abomination unto the Lord: but he loveth him that followeth after righteousness" (Proverbs 15:9).

28. "Then said one unto him, Lord, are there few that be saved?" (Luke 13:23).

29. "And she went and told them that had been with him, as they mourned and wept" (Mark 16:10).

30. "And they said unto him, Concerning Jesus of Nazareth, which was a prophet mighty in deed and word before God and all the people" (Luke 24:19).

TWO THINGS GRAMMATICALLY CONNECTED WITH A THIRD

1. "Jesus said unto them, If God were your Father, ye would love me: for I proceeded forth and came from God; neither came I of myself, but he sent me" (John 8:42). What is the "third thing," with which the others are connected? Is it the second *God* or is it *from God*? And what are the "two things?" Are they *proceeded forth* and *came from*? Or are they *proceeded forth* and *came*?

2. "For ye had compassion of me in my bonds, and took joyfully the spoiling of your goods, knowing in yourselves that ye have in heaven a better and an enduring substance" (Hebrews 10:34).

3. "And be not conformed to this world; but be ye transformed by the renewing of your mind, that ye may prove what is that good, and acceptable, and perfect, will of God" (Romans 12:2).

4. "The Lord is in his holy temple, the Lord's throne is in heaven: his eyes behold, his eyelids try, the children of men" (Psalm 11:4).

5. Any word you can leave out without changing the meaning you need not and should not stress.

6. ". . . grandsires, babies and old women,
Either past or not arrived to pith and puissance. . ."
—Shakespeare: *King Henry V.*

A CONNECTING WORD FOLLOWED BY A PARENTHETICAL EXPRESSION SET OFF BY COMMAS

1. "But God commendeth his love toward us, in that, while we

were yet sinners, Christ died for us " (Romans 5:8).

2. " Because that, when they knew God, they glorified him not as God, neither were thankful " (Romans 1:21).

3. " And it came to pass, that, while they communed together and reasoned, Jesus himself drew near, and went with them " (Luke 24:15).

4. " And he went forward a little, and fell on the ground, and prayed that, if it were possible, the hour might pass from him " (Mark 14:35).

5. " I find then a law, that, when I would do good, evil is present with me " (Romans 7:21).

6. " Only they see not God, I know,
Nor all that chivalry of His,
The soldier-saints who, row on row,

" Burn upward each to his point of bliss—
Since, the end of life being manifest,
He had burned his way thro' the world to this."—Browning: *The Statue and the Bust.*

7. " Friction, no doubt, there still occasionally was, for, while the Queen and the Prince devoted themselves to foreign politics as much as ever, their views, when the war was over, became once more antagonistic to those of the Prime Minister." Lytton Strachey: *Queen Victoria.**

8. " Indeed, with that deep and passionate conservatism which, to the very end of his incredible career, gave such an unexpected coloring to his inexplicable character, Mr. Gladstone viewed Victoria through a haze of awe which was almost religious."—*Ibid.*

9. ". . . she consulted Sir James Clark, the royal physician, and, after the consultation, Sir James let his tongue wag, too."— *Ibid.*

10. " It was in this spirit that, as Foreign Secretary, he watched over the interests of Englishmen abroad."—*Ibid.*

* Copyright, 1921, by Harcourt, Brace and Company, Inc. Quoted by permission.

11. " The public knew that it had in Lord Palmerstone **not** only a high-mettled master, but also a devoted servant—that he was, in every sense of the word, a public man."—*Ibid.*

12. " An important step was taken when, before the birth of the Princess Royal, the Prince, without any opposition in Parliament, was appointed Regent in case of the death of the Queen."—*Ibid.*

13. " And thus all Mr. Gladstone's zeal and devotion, his ceremonious phrases, his low bows, his punctilious correctitudes, were utterly wasted; and when, in the excess of his loyalty, he went further, and imputed to the object of his veneration, with obsequious blindness, the subtlety of intellect, the wide reading, the grave enthusiasm, which he himself possessed, the misunderstanding became complete."—*Ibid.*

VOCATIVES

1. " I beseech you therefore, brethren, by the mercies of God, that ye present your bodies a living sacrifice, holy, acceptable unto God, which is your reasonable service " (Romans 12:1).

2. " Grudge not one against another, brethren, lest ye be condemned " (James 5:9).

3. " Can the fig tree, my brethren, bear olive berries? " (James 3:12).

4. " For since the beginning of the world men have not heard, nor perceived by the ear, neither hath the eye seen, O God, beside thee, what he hath prepared for him that waiteth for him " (Isaiah 64:4).

5. " When ends life's transient dream,
When death's cold sullen stream
Shall o'er me roll,
Blest Saviour, then, in love,
Fear and distrust remove;
Oh bear me safe above—
A ransomed soul."—Lowell Mason: *My Faith Looks Up To Thee.*

6. "When other helpers fail, and comforts flee,
   Help of the helpless, oh, abide with me!"—W. H. Monk:
   Abide with Me.

7. "Deliver me, O Lord, from the evil man" (Psalm 140:1).

QUOTATIONS

1. The speaker declared that, when Washington urged this country to steer clear of "entangling alliances," he was not advocating what we today call isolationism.

EXTRACTING TWO IDEAS INSTEAD OF ONLY ONE

1. "And he had in his hand a little book open" (Revelation 10:2).

2. "And saying, Sirs, why do ye these things? We also are men of like passions with you" (Acts 14:15). (Study Acts 14: 8-18.)

WHAT DOES IT MODIFY OR BELONG WITH?

1. "And Ruth said, Intreat me not to leave thee, or to return from following after thee" (Ruth 1:16).

2. "Because that, when they knew God, they glorified him not as God, neither were thankful" (Romans 1:21).

3. "But now, after that ye have known God, or rather are known of God, how turn ye again to the weak and beggarly elements, whereunto ye desire again to be in bondage?" (Galatians 4:9).

4. "For ye have not received the spirit of bondage again to fear; but ye have received the Spirit of adoption, whereby we cry, Abba, Father" (Romans 8:15).

5. "And after eight days again his disciples were within, and Thomas was with them: then came Jesus, the doors being shut, and stood in the midst, and said, Peace be unto you" (John 20:26).

6. "Now when Jesus was risen early the first day of the week, he appeared first to Mary Magdalene, out of whom he had cast seven devils" (Mark 16:9).

7. "And she went and told them that had been with him, as they mourned and wept" (Mark 16:10).

8. "We are confident, I say, and willing rather to be absent from the body, and to be present with the Lord" (II Corinthians 5:8).

9. "And when they could not find by what way they might bring him in because of the multitude, they went upon the housetop, and let him down through the tiling with his couch into the midst before Jesus" (Luke 5:19).

10. "Now a certain man was sick, named Lazarus, of Bethany, the town of Mary and her sister Martha" (John 11:1).

11. "While yet he spake, there cometh one from the ruler of the synagogue's house, saying to him, Thy daughter is dead; trouble not the Master" (Luke 8:49).

12. "By faith Moses, when he was come to years, refused to be called the son of Pharaoh's daughter" (Hebrews 11:24).

13. "But seek ye first the kingdom of God, and his righteousness; and all these things shall be added unto you" (Matthew 6:33).

14. "While we look not at the things which are seen, but at the things which are not seen: for the things which are seen are temporal; but the things which are not seen are eternal" (II Corinthians 4:18).

15. "For we wrestle not against flesh and blood, but against principalities, against powers, against the rulers of the darkness of this world, against spiritual wickedness in high places" (Ephesians 6:12).

16. "Ye are of your father the devil, and the lusts of your father ye will do. He was a murderer from the beginning, and abode not in the truth, because there is no truth in him" (John 8:44).

17. "For thus said the Lord that created the heavens; God himself that formed the earth and made it; he hath established it, he created it not in vain, he formed it to be inhabited" (Isaiah 45:18).

18. "And Asa in the thirty and ninth year of his reign was diseased in his feet, until his disease was exceedingly great: yet in his disease he sought not to the Lord, but to the physicians" (II Chronicles 16:12).

19. "Forasmuch as ye are manifestly declared to be the epistle of Christ ministered by us, written not with ink, but with the Spirit of the living God; not in tables of stone, but in fleshy tables of the heart" (II Corinthians 3:3).

20. "I can of mine own self do nothing: as I hear, I judge: and my judgment is just; because I seek not mine own will, but the will of the Father which hath sent me" (John 5:30).

POETRY AND HYMNS

1. "Onward, Christian soldiers,
   Marching as to war;
   With the cross of Jesus,
   Going on before."—Sabine Baring-Gould.

2. "Weep no more, my lady,
   Oh! weep no more today!"—Stephen Foster.

TWO IDEAS IN CONJUNCTION

1. "For I was an hungred, and ye gave me meat: I was thirsty, and ye gave me drink: I was a stranger and ye took me in" (Matthew 25:35).
   "Naked, and ye clothed me: I was sick, and ye visited me: I was in prison, and ye came unto me" (Matthew 25:36).
   "Then shall the righteous answer him, saying, Lord, when saw we thee an hungered, and fed thee? or thirsty, and gave thee drink?" (Matthew 25:37).
   "When saw we thee a stranger, and took thee in? or naked, and clothed thee?" (Matthew 25:38).
   "Or when saw we thee sick, or in prison, and came unto thee?" (Matthew 25:39).

2. "They shall not build, and another inhabit; they shall not plant, and another eat: for as the days of a tree are the days of my people, and mine elect shall long enjoy the work of their hands" (Isaiah 65:22).

3. " They shall run, and not be weary; and they shall **walk, and** not faint " (Isaiah 40:31).

RESTRICTIVE AND NONRESTRICTIVE MODIFIERS

1. The clause, *that is sitting in the gold chair,* is a restrictive modifier of *man.* Therefore, you should not set it off by commas and you would not, in conversation, pause after *man.*

2. The participial modifier, *sitting in the gold chair,* is a restrictive modifier of *man.* Therefore, you should not set it off by commas and you would not, in conversation, pause after *man.*

3. The prepositional phrase, *in the gold chair,* is a restrictive modifier of *man.* Therefore, you should not set it off by commas and you would not, in conversation, pause after *man.*

4. *Who is sitting in the gold chair* is a nonrestrictive modifier of *President.* (It isn't necessary to restrict or identify " our President " as the man in the gold chair because presumably there is only one President.) Therefore, we naturally pause after *President* and should set off the nonrestrictive modifier with commas: Our President, who is sitting in the gold chair, is going to make a speech.

5. *Sitting in the gold chair* is a nonrestrictive modifier of *President.* Therefore, we naturally pause after *President* and should set off the nonrestrictive modifier with commas: Our President, sitting in the gold chair, is going to make a speech.

6. *In the gold chair* is a nonrestrictive modifier of *President.* Therefore, we naturally pause after *President* and should set off the nonrestrictive modifier with commas: Our President, in the gold chair, is going to make a speech.

7. *We've been looking for* (equal to *that we've been looking for*) is a restrictive modifier of *man.* The punctuation is correct.

8. *That found a wallet* is a restrictive modifier of *person*. The punctuation is correct.

9. *Whose novels I have enjoyed for years* is a nonrestrictive modifier of *author*. It should be punctuated like this: That author, whose novels I have enjoyed for years, has recently written a book of essays.

10. This is punctuated correctly, as "called *The Man He Killed*" is a restrictive modifier of *poem*.

11. This map, which is ten years old, has a number of inaccuracies. (This punctuation is the correct one, since *which is ten years old* modifies *map* nonrestrictively.)

12. *Whom I haven't seen for fifteen years* is a nonrestrictive modifier of *brother*. Since you can have only one twin brother, there is no need to restrict *twin brother* to the one you haven't seen for fifteen years. I am going to call on my twin brother, whom I haven't seen for fifteen years.

13. Recast this into prose order: She speaks a various language to him who holds communion with her visible forms in the love of nature. *Who holds communion with her visible forms* is a restrictive modifier of *him* and, therefore, does not need to be set off by commas. (In some editions, commas are shown after *who, nature, forms;* in others, there is a comma after *forms* only. This is just another proof that you should never rely on the punctuation for your phrasing.)

14. In prose order this would read: She watched the square like a book holding one picture and only one, which she daily undertook to find. *Holding one picture and only one* is a restrictive modifier of *book* and so does not need to be set off by commas. *Which daily to find she undertook* is a nonrestrictive modifier of the second *one* and, therefore, needs to be separated from the second *one* by a comma, as Browning wrote it:

> " And she—she watched the square like a book
> Holding one picture and only one,
> Which daily to find she undertook."

15. Hebrews 11:6. *That cometh to God* is a restrictive modifier of *he; that diligently seek him* is a restrictive modifier of *them.* Most readers handle the first one correctly, with no pause between *he* and *that,* but many illogically pause after *them.*

16. Hebrews 11:10. *Which hath foundations* is a restrictive modifier of *city* and should not be preceded by a pause; but neither position, meaning, nor punctuation indicates unmistakably whether *whose builder and maker is God* is a restrictive or a nonrestrictive modifier of *city.* It doesn't matter, anyway, as it's so far from *city* that you couldn't indicate it by pausing.

17. Job 14:1. The punctuation here shows that *that is born of a woman* is a restrictive modifier of *man* and this makes all the difference in the meaning here.

18. Luke 7:47. *Which are many* is a nonrestrictive modifier of *sins.*

19. Psalms 138:8. Almost everyone reads this correctly, since *which concerneth me* is so obviously a restrictive modifier of *that.*

20. Genesis 2:8. Here again, as in Exercise 17, it makes a great deal of difference in the sense to see that *whom he had formed* is a restrictive modifier of *man.* (Do you like a slight emphasis on the second *he?*)

21. James 5:1. *That shall come upon you* modifies *miseries* restrictively.

22. II Corinthians 4:6. You would pause after *God,* since *who commanded the light to shine out of darkness* is a nonrestrictive modifier of *God.*

23. Luke 5:18. Don't pause after *man,* as *which was taken with a palsy* is a restrictive modifier of *man.*

24. Genesis 49:1. *Which shall befall you in the last days* is a restrictive modifier of the second *that;* so naturally you won't pause between the second *that* and *which.*

25. Genesis 49:8. *Whom thy brethren shall praise* modifies *he* restrictively; so don't pause between *he* and *whom.*

26. Malachi 3:1. *Whom ye seek* is a nonrestrictive modifier of *Lord* and *whom ye delight in* is a nonrestrictive modifier of *messenger.* So you will pause between *Lord* and *whom;* and you can't connect *whom ye delight in* with its antecedent, *messenger,* as they are separated by three words. You wouldn't want to, since *whom ye delight in* is a nonrestrictive modifier.

27. Proverbs 15:9. Make no pause between *him* and *that,* since *that followeth after righteousness* modifies *him* restrictively.

28. Luke 13:23. Don't pause between *few* and *that,* as *that be saved* is a restrictive modifier of *few.*

29. Mark 16:10. *That had been with him* is a restrictive modifier of *them;* so don't pause between *them* and *that.* You do hear a pause here frequently, however, sometimes because the reader is not thinking about restrictive and nonrestrictive modifiers and their significance and sometimes because he needs a pause somewhere among all these words and doesn't know any better place to take one. It would be better to pause very slightly before *them* or after *went.* (Incidentally, be sure to pause after *him,* or you will make *as they mourned and wept* sound as if it modified *had been with him* instead of *told.* It doesn't mean that they mourned and wept as they were with him; it means they mourned and wept as she told them.)

30. Luke 24:19. Make a slight pause after *Nazareth,* as *which was a prophet mighty in deed and word before God and all the people* is a modifier of *Jesus,* not of *Nazareth.*

TWO THINGS GRAMMATICALLY CONNECTED WITH A THIRD

1. John 8:42. If the "third thing" is the second *God,* then the sentence would mean "I proceeded forth God and came from God." Since this does not make sense, we see that the "third thing" is *from God,* because it means "I proceeded

forth from God and came from God." So the two things connected with *from God* are: *proceeded forth* and *came*.

2. Hebrews 10:34. *Better* and *enduring* both modify *substance*. The construction here is so simple that you needn't make long pauses after *better* and *enduring*. One brief pause before *substance* and slight stress on *enduring* will make the meaning clear. (Do not make a pause after *better* with no pause after *enduring*.)

3. Romans 12:2. You have three things (*good, acceptable,* and *perfect*) connected with a fourth (*will of God*). Try a good pause before *will of God*.

4. Psalm 11:4. This is made very easy for the reader by the very convenient commas (correctly placed, too). You don't refer to them for your phrasing, remember; you refer to them for the grammatical construction. From that you get your meaning. From the meaning you decide on your phrasing. Probably you will pause slightly after *behold* and after *try*.

5. The word *stress* is the third thing, with which *need not* and *should not* are connected. You may or may not pause after the first *not* but you should pause after the second *not*. Also, emphasize *should*. The worst way to read this is to pause after the first *not,* subdue *should,* and make no pause after the second *not*. This leaves the hearer wondering: " Need not what? "

6. Do you pause after *arrived* or after *to?* The easiest way is to find out what the " first thing " connects with. Then the break should come before that word, which is the " third thing." In this sentence *past* is the " first thing." It is not " past to pith and puissance " but " past pith and puissance." So *arrived to,* not just *arrived,* is the " second thing " and *pith and puissance* the " third thing." You may or may not pause after *to*. You must not pause after *arrived*. Probably you would pause slightly after *to* and hold *to*.

But remember that the commas don't cause you to pause. Both punctuation and phrasing are effects, not causes. The meaning is the cause of the punctuation and of the phrasing. The punctuation then shows the meaning to the eye of the silent reader and the phrasing imparts the meaning to the ear of the listener.

A CONNECTING WORD FOLLOWED BY A PARENTHETICAL
EXPRESSION SET OFF BY COMMAS

1. Romans 5:8. If you want to give your hearers the impression that you are reading printed words aloud and going strictly according to the punctuation, just hold on to *that* and pause before *while.* But if you wish to sound as if you were just talking, subdue *that* to *th't* (not *thut*) and make no pause at all between *that* and *while.* (*That* is the connecting word and *while we were yet sinners* is the parenthetical expression.)

2. Romans 1:21. Do as you like about pausing before *that,* but take care not to hold or stress *that* and not to make any pause between *that* and *when.* (*That* is the connecting word and *when they knew God* is the parenthetical expression.)

3. Luke 24:15. You may ignore both the comma before *that* and the comma after *that;* but in order to sound conversational, you **must** ignore the comma **after** *that* and subdue *that.* (*That* is the connecting word and *while they communed together and reasoned* is the parenthetical expression.) You may logically pause before *that,* instead of ignoring the comma.

4. Mark 14:35. Be sure to soft-pedal *that* and do not pause between *that* and *if.* (*That* is the connecting word and *if it were possible* is the parenthetical expression.)

5. Romans 7:21. Subdue *that* and do not pause between *that* and *when.* (*That* is the connecting word and *when I would do good* is the parenthetical expression.)

6. *Who* is the connecting word and *row on row* is the parenthetical expression. If you think that *who burn upward each to his point of bliss* is a restrictive modifier of *soldier-saints,* as Browning's punctuation indicates, you will not pause before *who.* Of course, you will subdue *who* and not pause between *who* and the first *row.* The sense allows you to pause

or not after the second *row,* but you probably will need to pause there to breathe, as otherwise the phrase would be rather long. In reading anything as highly involved as Browning it is a good idea to pause more often than you otherwise would, so that your listeners can follow you better.

7. *For* is the connecting word and *while the Queen and the Prince devoted themselves to foreign politics as much as ever* is the parenthetical expression. Therefore, subdue *for* and make no pause between *for* and *while.*

8. An amateurish reader would be almost sure to hold the connecting word, *which,* and pause carefully for the comma before first *to.* One who had studied the way people really say this construction would do the very opposite. (*Which* is the connecting word and *to the very end of his incredible career* is the parenthetical expression.)

9. As a rule there would be no reason for holding the connecting word, *and,* in such a construction and pausing for the comma following *and.* Subdue *and* and don't pause before *after.* (*After the consultation* is the parenthetical expression.)

10. Soft-pedal the connecting word, *that,* and make no pause between *that* and the parenthetical expression, *as Foreign Secretary.*

11. Although *was* is not a connecting word in the sense that *which, that,* and *who* are connecting words, this construction should be read in the same way. Leave out the parenthetical expression (*in every sense of the word*) and you won't stress *was;* so, don't stress *was* when you include the parenthetical expression and don't pause after *was.*

12. *When* is a word seldom emphasized in conversation; therefore, it seldom should be emphasized in reading aloud. Read this sentence without the parenthetical expression (*before the birth of the Princess Royal*) and you will agree that you wouldn't stress *when.* So don't stress or hold *when,* even when you read the parenthetical expression after it, and don't pause before the parenthetical expression. (The reason that you stress *Prince* and pause after it, even though *Prince*

is followed by a parenthetical expression set off by commas, is that *Prince* is not a connecting word.)

13. The same thing applies here but this sentence is a bit harder to read without stressing *when*. In the sentence in Exercise 12 *when* is immediately preceded by a strong word, *taken,* on which you can rest your emphasis; but in this sentence *when* is immediately preceded by a weak word, *and,* and there is no word before *excess* which you can sensibly emphasize. (*When* is the connecting word and *in the excess of his loyalty* is the parenthetical expression.)

VOCATIVES

1. Romans 12:1. Surely nobody would read this with a pause before *brethren* and no pause before *by*. It is hardly necessary to suggest that you make no pause at all before *brethren*. You will probably feel that a slight pause after *brethren* sounds natural.

2. James 5:9. Surely nobody would read this with a pause before *brethren* and no pause before *lest*. It is hardly necessary to suggest that you make no pause at all before *brethren*. You will probably feel that a slight pause after *brethren* sounds natural.

3. James 3:12. Surely nobody would read this with a pause before *my brethren* and no pause before *bear*. It is hardly necessary to suggest that you make no pause at all before *my brethren*. You will probably feel that a slight pause after *my brethren* sounds natural.

4. Isaiah 64:4. The vocative, *O God,* would naturally cling to what precedes it, *seen,* without a pause. You will probably want to pause before *beside*.

5. Because of the pronounced rhythm and rhyme we hear this read with a decided pause before *Blest Saviour,* although this is a vocative and would naturally go with what precedes it. Now recast these lines into prose order: When life's transient dream ends, when death's cold sullen stream shall roll over me, Blest Saviour, then remove fear and distrust in

love: Oh, bear me (a ransomed soul) safe above. **If you can** forget the way you have always heard these lines read and sung, won't you agree that the pause should come after and not before *Blest Saviour,* whether you're reading the prose paraphrase or Lowell Mason's poem?

6. Almost always this is read as it must be sung, with a long pause before *Help* and almost none after *helpless.* Yet *Help of the helpless* is a vocative, and, therefore, should go with what precedes it. It may sound strange at first to read it with a pause after *helpless* and none before *Help* but that is the way it would be phrased if it were being said or thought for the first time instead of read aloud after years of hearing it said in the rhythmical way.

   A rather different kind of mistake is made in reading the titles and the first lines of two other familiar hymns. "Nearer, My God, to Thee" is usually read all together, like one word, because it has become so crystallized in our thought. But stop to think of the meaning and you will see that perhaps you should drop your voice slightly on *My God* (a vocative) and pause a short moment before *to Thee.* "Lead, Kindly Light" most people read like one word, usually stressing *Kindly.* But isn't *Kindly Light* a vocative? Then wouldn't you naturally lower your voice a bit on *Kindly,* instead of raising it? You would also naturally use rising inflection on *My God* and *Kindly Light.*

   These suggestions are made with respect, both for the hymns themselves and for the readers of them. Many readers hesitate to surprise their hearers by reading familiar verse and hymns in the manner indicated. Also, it is hard to conceive of such familiar and revered lines as ever having been said spontaneously for the first time. But if you agree that you would say, " Come-in-Louise—and sit down," and if you see the similarity of the grammatical constructions, you will surely agree that the suggested phrasings are the natural ones.

7. *O Lord,* the vocative, naturally goes with what precedes it.

QUOTATIONS

1. If you pause before *entangling,* you make your listeners see
    quotation marks rather than your meaning.

EXTRACTING TWO IDEAS INSTEAD OF ONLY ONE

1. Revelation 10:2. Frequently these ten words are read with
    no pause or with a pause before *a* and nowhere else, and
    with the only emphasis on *book.* This calls attention to *book,*
    which is proper, but it misses the opportunity to give two
    important ideas. If you pause very definitely after *book* and
    then stress *open* as much as *book* or even more, you impress
    upon your hearers not only the existence of the book but the
    fact that it was open, not closed.

2. Acts 14:15. Usually the first nine words of the second sen-
    tence of this verse are read without a pause and without
    much stress before *you.* But see how much meaning is lost
    by this reading. It is important that they were "of like
    passions," granted; but how much more important it is to
    bring out the fact that they were **men.** The people thought
    that they were gods but they were trying to assure them that
    they were not gods but merely men, like themselves. The fact
    that they were "of like passions" or feelings was secondary
    to and caused by the fact that they were men. Therefore, if
    you agree with this meaning, which seems obvious, you can
    bring it out by stressing *men* heavily and making a rather
    long pause after *men.* Many persons, on first hearing it read
    in this way, have said that they had never seen the full
    meaning in it before.

WHAT DOES IT MODIFY OR BELONG WITH?

1. Ruth 1:16. Naomi had just advised Ruth to return to her
    own people; so Ruth wasn't saying, "Intreat me that I
    should not leave you." She was saying, "Do not intreat me
    that I should leave you." Is there any reason, then, for
    pausing before *not?* You may either make no pause before
    or after *not,* or you may, better, make a small pause after

not. Just be sure not to pause before *not* with no pause after that word.

2. Romans 1:21. It is clearer to pause between *not* and *as* but it is not necessary. Just be sure not to pause before *not,* because this would sound as if you were going to say " not as God but as something else."

3. Galatians 4:9. Does the second *again* go with *desire* or with *to be in bondage?* If you believe the former, then pause after *again* and not before *again.* If you believe it goes with *to be in bondage,* pause before *again* and not after *again.* If you find a passage like this where you really cannot tell which it goes with, you can always read it so that it could go with either one, by making no pause either before or after the word in question. However, it is much better to understand a thing so clearly that you can tell where each idea belongs and usually it is possible to be sure.

4. Romans 8:15. If this means " ye have not received again the spirit of bondage," pause after *again* and not before *again.* If it means " ye have not received the spirit of bondage to fear again," pause before *again* and not after *again.*

5. If you make no pause between *days* and *again* and do make a pause after *again,* you imply that they have once before assembled after an eight-day interlude and are now assembling again after another eight-day interlude. But if it means that again the disciples were within, after eight days, you will pause before *again* and not before *his.*

6. If *risen* means " arose from bed," you will pause after *early* but not after *risen.* If it means *resurrected* or *ascended,* you will pause before *early* and not after *early.* The placing of the pause before or after *early* changes the sense completely.

7. The punctuation here tells you the meaning (that *as they mourned and wept* goes with *told* and not with *had been with them*) and the meaning in turn tells you how to phrase it. It cannot be repeated too often that the punctuation does not tell you how to phrase. You are pausing after *him,* not because there is a comma there, but because there is no

close connection between *had been with him* and *as they mourned and wept*. It does not mean " had been with him as they mourned and wept "; it means " went and told them as they mourned and wept."

8. Frequently, if not usually, this is read with *rather* closely connected with *willing* and with a pause after *rather*. But does it really mean " rather willing " or " willing rather " ? Doesn't it mean " rather to be absent from the body, etc." ? If so, you would pause before *rather* and not after *rather*. However, because of the arrangement of this whole sentence, pausing noticeably before *rather* might make it sound like two things grammatically connected with a third; that is, it might sound as if both *confident* and *willing* were connected with *rather to be absent, etc*. So it is perhaps better here not to make too much of a pause before *rather* but to be sure not to pause at all after *rather*.

9. If you were relying on commas to tell you where to pause, you would give a misleading meaning here. Even though there is no comma between *in* and *because* you pause there, because it means not " bring him in because of the multitude " but " could not find because of the multitude."

10. Even though there is a comma after *sick* and even though the sense clearly calls for a slight pause after *sick*, we sometimes hear this read with no pause at all after *sick*. This gives the effect of " sick-named-Lazarus."

11. Surely no one would phrase this passage wrong but it is interesting because it shows how a pause in the wrong place can alter the meaning. If you pause after *ruler* it sounds as if one came from the ruler—of the synagogue's house. This, of course, makes no sense. So you don't pause at all after *ruler*. You can make a very slight pause after *synagogue's* or you can hesitate on or hold the last syllable of *synagogue's*. This shows that it means that one came from the house—of the ruler of the synagogue.

12. If you pause after *son* it means Pharaoh's grandson; if you make no pause at all after *son* and pause after *Pharaoh's* or

hesitate on the last syllable of *Pharaoh's,* it means Pharaoh's granddaughter, which, of course, is wrong.

13. This is like the passage about the tares. It does not say, " Seek first this and then that "; it says, " First seek." So you should be careful not to pause before *first;* you probably but not necessarily would pause after *first.*

14. This is not saying, " We do not look at the things, etc." It says, " We look not at this but at that." Since *not* goes not with *look* but with what follows, be careful not to pause after *not.*

15. This is a typical " not-so-and-so-but-such-and-such " construction. *Not* does not modify *wrestle;* it goes with what follows, balancing the *but.* Be sure not to pause after *not* but you may do as you like about pausing before *not.*

16. This is not a " not-so-and-so-but-such-and-such " construction. It means, " did not abide in the truth "; therefore, you will not pause before *not.* Readers are less likely to phrase incorrectly in a construction like this than in the one in Exercise 15. That is, those who do not know how to figure out the correct phrasing tend to pause after the *not* every time rather than before.

17. To pause on the wrong side of the *not* seriously impairs the meaning. If you pause after *not,* you say He did not create it, which, of course, is not the meaning. *Not* does not go with *created;* it goes with *in vain.* But be sure not to pause after *not;* a short pause before *not* helps to make it perfectly clear.

18. This is another " not-so-and-so-but-such-and-such " construction. *Not* goes with what follows and you should be careful not to pause after *not.*

19. This is a " not-so-and-so-but-such-and-such " construction: " not with ink but with the Spirit of the living God." Therefore, make no pause after *not.*

20. This is a " not-so-and-so-but-such-and-such " construction: " not mine own will but the will of the Father." Make no pause after *not.*

POETRY AND HYMNS

1. Because the first three words form the title of this hymn, the first line is usually read like one word and with a falling inflection and with a complete stop following them. But *Christian soldiers* is a vocative and should, therefore, be read in a lower tone and with a rising inflection. You would read *Christian soldiers* as you would *my friends* in this sentence: Forward, my friends, and face the foe.

2. Because of the way the familiar music stresses these words, people usually read them with heavy emphasis on *lady*. But *my lady* is a vocative and, therefore, would naturally be spoken without so much stress and with a rising inflection.

TWO IDEAS IN CONJUNCTION

1. In verse 37, don't pause after *hungred* or *thirsty*. Don't pause after *stranger* or *naked* in verse 38 or after *sick* or *in prison* in verse 39. They're not asking merely when they saw him hungry or thirsty; they're not asking merely when they saw him a stranger, naked, sick, or in prison. They're asking when certain things happened together or in conjunction. When did they see-him-hungry-and-feed-him? When did they see-him-thirsty-and-give-him-drink? See-him-a-stranger-and-take-him-in? See-him-naked-and-clothe-him? See-him-sick-or-in-prison-and-come-unto-him? It's almost as if they had asked when they ever fed him when he was hungry.

2. This does not say, "They shall not build." It amounts to saying, "They shall not build fruitlessly." Unless the second idea, expressed in *and another inhabit,* is read without separation from the first idea, the meaning of the whole verse is seriously altered.

VI

HOW TO READ THE BIBLE

Some Generalities

The whole purpose of this chapter is to help you to read the Bible naturally and meaningfully.

The Bible is one of the most difficult of books to read aloud, first, because it really is difficult, having archaic language and constructions and words different from ours today, and, second, because we make it difficult to read. Most readers of the Bible are properly reverent and many even become over-awed and try so hard to put reverence into their reading, instead of just letting their genuine reverence show itself naturally, that their efforts result in unpleasant straining and affectation.

The two main faults of Bible readers are monotonous or colorless reading and affected or overly dramatic reading. Although the latter is by far the more prevalent and objectionable, let us first consider the former fault: colorless reading.

The colorless reader may have a naturally monotonous voice, with little variety or range. If this is his trouble, he should work with a good teacher of the speaking voice, as printed pages cannot be expected to remove this difficulty. More frequently, however, monotonous reading is the result of not knowing how to phrase and emphasize so as to let out the meanings he sees. In that case this book should be of great help, if used step by step. Quite as often, however, colorless reading results from a deliberate and well-meant attempt to avoid what is blanketed under the term " interpretation."

Webster's New International Dictionary, Second Edition, defines the verb *to interpret* as:

" 1. To explain or tell the meaning of; to translate into intelligible or familiar language or terms; to expound; elucidate; translate;—applied especially to language, but also to dreams, signs, conduct, mysteries, etc.
    'Emmanuel, which being *interpreted* is, God with us.' Matt. 1:23.

" 2. To understand or appreciate in the light of individual belief, judgment, or interest; construe; as, to *interpret* actions, intentions, contracts.

" 3. To apprehend and represent by means of art; to show by illustrative representation; as, an actor *interprets* a character; a musician, a sonata; an artist, a landscape."

The third definition is the one that applies most nearly to what an oral reader is trying to do for his audience. It does not mean personal interpretation, which is different from legitimate interpretation.

There is only one way to keep from "interpreting" and that is to refrain from any sort of phrasing or emphasis, to read in a level, uninflected monotone, with no pause from the beginning of each sentence to the end. The moment you stress one word more than another or even stop in a long sentence to catch your breath, you are "interpreting," if you wish to call it that. Unless you read everything in a dull and meaningless chant, therefore, you will be giving out some meaning or other. If you stress this word, you imply one meaning; if you stress that word, you imply something else.

Isn't it a good idea, then, to settle upon the obvious meaning of a passage and then study ways to phrase and emphasize in order to let this meaning come out, rather than to stumble along and sometimes unintentionally bring out meanings that are wrong and that you don't intend to bring out?

There is such a thing, though, as really officious and blameworthy interpreting. Sometimes readers decide that they want a Bible passage to mean a certain thing and then give an outlandish twist to the phrasing or emphasis, frequently reading one part of speech as if it were a different one, as by making a conjunction sound like a

preposition. This is downright personal interpretation and has nothing in common with the principles set forth in this book.

We all use " interpretation," whether we realize it or not; that is,
if our reading has any understanding and meaning in it at all, we
are always deliberately phrasing after one word and not after
another, emphasizing one word and not another. And the thoughtful reader phrases and emphasizes the same way every time he
reads the same passage, instead of reading it first one way and then
another, in a hit-or-miss fashion. (Of course, if there is more than
one way to read a passage with the correct meaning, he may read
it different ways at different times, for variety. Or, if he concludes
that his phrasing and stress have been wrong, he will, of course,
change.) See how phrasing makes all the difference in the meaning
of Psalm 13:4: " Lest mine enemy say, I have prevailed against
him . . ." Surely this obviously means: Lest mine enemy say that he
(my enemy) has prevailed against me. This meaning can be indicated only by a long pause between *say* and *I*. If it is read without
intelligent phrasing (with no pause between *say* and *I*), it is made
to mean exactly the opposite of the true sense: Lest mine enemy say
that I have prevailed against him (my enemy). Can this obviously
correct placing of a pause be called "interpreting"?

Consider Ephesians 4:8: " Wherefore he saith, When he ascended up on high, he led captivity captive, and gave gifts unto
men." Unless you read the first thirteen words with no pause and
with little emphasis, you are bound to " interpret " it one way or
the other. But isn't it perfectly clear, even before you consult
Moffatt's translation or the Greek text, that " When he ascended up
on high " goes with " he led captivity captive " and not with
" Wherefore he saith "? Does it make sense, then, to pause after
high and fail to pause after *saith?* And is it personal interpretation
to read it so as to bring out the unmistakable meaning, by pausing
decidedly after *saith* and pausing only slightly or not at all after
high? If, in a conscientious attempt to avoid personal interpretation, you use no pauses at all, aren't you personally interpreting by
deliberately hiding the obvious meaning?

Probably nobody reads this passage without pausing after *saith*
and nobody calls such phrasing " interpretation." And yet a few

may object to intelligent phrasing and emphasizing in other places which are less nearly uniformly read, calling it interpretation.

" And when they had fulfilled the days, as they returned, the child Jesus tarried behind in Jerusalem " (Luke 2:43). Did they fulfill the days as they returned? Or did Jesus tarry behind as they returned? If you make no pause after *days* and a long pause after *returned,* aren't you deliberately interpreting with the wrong meaning? But, if you pause long after *days* and only slightly if at all after *returned,* aren't you just impersonally letting the obvious meaning bring itself out?

You may believe that your listeners will understand the meaning no matter how you phrase and emphasize, because everybody is familiar with the Bible. Some are; some aren't. Those who are will be annoyed by your wrong stress and pauses; those who aren't need to have it presented clearly. A clear presentation is needed especially in reading the less familiar verses.

Often readers are puzzled over the exact meaning of some word or phrase in the King James version, because English is not an exact language. In Revelation 4:11 you might not know whether *are* and *were created* are two different verbs (forms of *to be* and of *to create*) or merely two different tenses of the same verb, *to create*. (". . . For thou hast created all things, and for thy pleasure they are and were created.") If it is two tenses of *to create,* it means " for thy pleasure they are created and were created " and you would read it: " for thy pleasure they are and were created." (You might stress *are* and you would certainly stress *were,* since *were* is contrasted with *are,* and you would perhaps pause before *created,* as the third thing with which the two things, *are* and *were,* are grammatically connected.) But if *are* is part of the verb *to be* instead of the verb *to create,* then the passage doesn't mean " for thy pleasure they are created and were created "; it means " for thy pleasure they exist and were created," and you would slightly stress *are,* pause after *are,* subdue *were,* make no pause after *were,* and stress *created.*

Now which way will you read it? The two meanings are not the same. It means either one thing or the other. Are you going to bring out the right meaning? You will be interpreting. Are you going to bring out the wrong meaning? You will be personally interpreting. Personal interpretation should be wholly avoided.

Numerous instances like this arise in reading the Bible. Some students can turn to the Greek or the Hebrew and can usually tell which of the possible meanings suggested by the English is authentic, since these languages are more nearly exact than English. Many passages expressed in English will be ambiguous but their Greek renditions will be marvels of exactitude. However, most Bible students do not know Hebrew or Greek and many like to use one or several of the recognized modern, nondenominational translations to settle the questions. (You may look up Revelation 4:11 for yourself in one of these translations and see which phrasing and emphasis are correct.)

You may say at this point that this is involving too much process. It does require some process, but you had to use process to learn the alphabet and to learn to read at the outset. So you need still more process, perhaps, to help you to learn to read intelligently. Remember that musicians and singers have to use process to learn their techniques, too. It is better to use process and read well than not to use it and read poorly.

The first necessity is inspirational, to feel the spirit of the passage. The second is technical. Stressing the second and neglecting the first results in cold, fruitless, uninspiring reading. An abundance of the first with none of the second lets your hearers know that you feel the spirit of the passage but don't know how to give the meaning of it.

Much more annoying to most listeners than colorless reading, however, is "fancy" reading or reading that has mannerisms. Monotonous reading at least is usually sincere, but mannered and overly dramatic reading sometimes gives the impression of insincerity. And the more often and the longer the listeners hear this sort of reading, the more unpleasant it grows. Many agree that they would rather listen to an untutored reader who makes honest mistakes than to a "trained" reader who reads affectedly or ornately.

Mannerisms are out of place in a reader of the Bible especially, as they personalize the reading, causing the hearers to be conscious of the reader more than of the reading.

It is impossible to enumerate all the mannerisms to be avoided.

One is the tendency to begin all sentences on a high pitch and then come down. In expressions like "O Lord" and "O God," used often in the Bible, some readers start with a high pitch on *O* and then drop on the second word. This makes it sound like a lament or an interjection rather than like a vocative, a word addressing the Lord, often in praise rather than in lamentation.

Another mannerism heard among readers of the Bible is an excessive sweetness. Approach your Bible-reading with reverence, of course, but don't try so hard to sound reverent that you end, as many Bible readers do, by sounding melancholy, sanctimonious, or mournful. Some Bible-reading sounds so resigned that it gives the effect of just one prolonged sigh. Many oral readers of the Bible don't read it at all: they sing it or coo it or sob it.

On the other hand, it is just as bad to try to sound "joyful." Don't try to put joy into your reading. If you feel the inspiration and joy that you should feel in what you are reading, it will reveal itself of its own accord. But if you consciously try to "register" joy, as many readers (of the Bible, inspirational verse, etc.) do, you are likely to produce a grotesque effect that you yourself will never suspect. As a rule, only trained actors can depend on being able to register joy or any other emotion as they desire, and deliberate dramatics has no place in Bible-reading. True joy comes from within and will show itself without any effort on your part. Do not try to apply it to your words deliberately.

Here are some more things to avoid. Don't try to sound soothing or sweet. Many Bible readers, especially on the radio, sound so syrupy that you feel as if they should start each sentence with: "Now, dear little children . . ." And don't fix a set smile on your face. Even over the radio this will "show." Just look pleasant and try to feel comfortable (hard advice to follow!), neither grim nor too sweet. Don't plead.

Don't allow yourself to dramatize or to read too emotionally. For example, don't act out words like "lift up" or "glorify" or "rejoice" or "triumph" by raising your pitch or your inflection— or your head. Some readers say that, if you just feel what you are reading, your phrasing and emphasis will automatically arrange themselves to bring out the meaning. This is about like saying that, if you feel a beautiful hymn, you can play it on the pipe organ without first working hard with technicalities.

Oversustaining of the vowels is singing, not talking. It is unnatural and is responsible for much of the affectedly intoned or " sung " reading of the Bible. Some readers hold the idea that negative or unpleasant words should be subdued and only affirmative or pleasant words emphasized. The objection to this is that frequently the negations are almost as important as the positive statements. If you always followed this policy of slighting negatives, in reading the twentieth chapter of Exodus you would suppress one of the most important passages in the Old Testament, since eight of the Ten Commandments and half of a ninth are negative.

Sometimes you hear that every pronoun referring to God or to Jesus should be emphasized and that to fail to do this is irreverent. We don't do this in spontaneous speech. To see what a peculiar effect such a practice brings about, read Matthew 8:23, emphasizing the pronouns that refer to Jesus (*he, his,* and *him*) : " And when he was entered into a ship, his disciples followed him."

Never try to make rules about how to read. Not artificial rules but common sense and a trained ear make good reading.

If you approach your reading with the right attitude and then keep your thought on the meaning of the passage, you will bring out the right significance with the desired effect.

Don't labor. Once you feel sure of the meaning of a passage, read it as you would if it were not in the Bible. Just try to bring out the logical thought. In order to do this, it is sometimes necessary to try to forget the way you have heard a familiar and beautiful passage read all your life and see it as if for the first time. Don't strive to " put in "; when professional actors are forced to appear in an inferior play, they sometimes have to add to the flat lines by their clever inflections and stage business but the Bible does not need to have anything " put in." All it needs is to have its meaning brought out or let out.

A frequent fault among Bible readers is overconscientiousness, shown, for instance, in emphasizing too many words. Sometimes readers seem to have the idea that every word in a Bible verse is so important, because of its sacred nature, that it must not be slighted.

They produce the same effect as those who, through mistaken dread of interpretation, try to use no emphasis at all: utter colorlessness and meaninglessness. It is as if da Vinci had put no shadows or dark colors into his painting of *The Last Supper*. If everything had been painted bright, the figures of the people would have been in-distinguishable from the unimportant objects.

Akin to the practice of emphasizing too many words is the idea that one must read very slowly. This does not make one sound more reverent; nor does it make it easier for people to understand. It usually sounds more mournful than reverent; and it is not necessary in order to be understood. In fact, it often makes the reading harder to follow. Instead of plodding slowly through each word in a sentence, the effective reader gives out a phrase rather rapidly and then pauses to let the hearer catch up; then he reads the next phrase and again pauses, etc. Thus, it takes him about the same amount of time to read a given passage as it does the one that reads the whole thing at a uniform rate of slowness with few noticeable pauses. But the latter has no rhythm and variety and considerably less meaning. It would be a very unsatisfactory train that went very slowly over its whole route, never coming to a complete stop at stations and never increasing speed between them. We want a train to go fast but to stop and wait as long as necessary at each station.

It may seem surprising that excessive slowness of reading has been mentioned instead of excessive rapidity. Although there is probably as much of one as of the other, slowness was warned against first, because few readers are aware that they read too slowly while most readers are under the impression that they read too fast. And most readers, especially beginners, do read too fast. The best way to remedy this is the same method that was recommended for the opposite fault. Instead of trying to slow down on every word, decide on good places to pause and select plenty of them. Then be sure to pause at each of these places. Pause a good while at each stopping-place and do not pause between them or try to read very slowly between them. Read each phrase fairly fast, if you like, but be sure to pause often and pause at the same places every time you read the passage.

Many otherwise good readers believe that as soon as they start to read the Bible, particularly from a platform, they must dramatize and must exaggerate their pronunciation and articulation to the point of orating and laboring. Let common sense and good taste be your guides. Naturally, both because of the sacred and formal nature of what you are reading, and because of reading to a larger group and in a larger room, you will need to speak a little more distinctly and a little more slowly. But you should not use wholly different pronunciations from your informal talking and you should not intone. This is true especially of Bible-reading over the radio.

In the ancient Greek theater the actors enlarged their faces by wearing big masks and increased their stature by wearing high buskins. Today actors do not go to such extremes; but they do not use just street make-up either, as their audiences would not be able to make out their features and expressions. They follow a middle, and sensible, course by accentuating their natural features with modern stage make-up. Similarly, a public reader, especially of the Bible, should not make himself inaudible by using the completely relaxed, indistinct type of conversational speaking but should not go to the opposite extreme of affectedly " singing " his words.

Words ending in *-ness, -ed, -es,* etc. are usually the victims of this tendency to exaggerate pronunciation and articulation. These words have two sets of pronunciation, recognized in Webster. They are what might be called a " sitting-down " pronunciation and a " standing-up " pronunciation. Webster says: " These words vary in pronunciation of the e from ĕ to ĭ. . . . The ĕ sound is often heard in deliberate or formal speech, but ĭ in more familiar speech, some speakers using ĭ in both styles."

Since the use of the short e in these suffixes is a decidedly formal type of pronunciation, wouldn't common sense and good taste argue that it should be used only by someone whose natural, every-day diction is of the most cultivated and formal type? But even these rare speakers do not use this type of pronunciation in conversation or even, as a rule, in formal speaking, as you can discover for yourself if you will listen to recordings of broadcasts of such speakers as Winston Churchill or Franklin Roosevelt. Even the Harvard accent, usually considered the most formal and cultivated type of American speech, does not include this use of the short e in these suffixes. Cer-

tainly it sounds out-of-place and unnatural in the reading of someone whose diction otherwise needs some improvement.

Almost anyone, sitting down and conversing informally, in saying
this sentence, " We appreciated your kindness in sending Alice's
roses," would pronounce it this way: " We appreciatid your kind-
niss in sending Aliciz roziz." But just let the same person stand up
and read this sentence from a printed page to an audience and the
chances are fairly numerous, especially if he is an amateur or a self-
conscious reader, that he will pronounce the last syllables with short
e's instead of with the more natural short *i's:* " We appreciat-edd
your kind-ness in sending Alic-ezz roz-ezz."

The dangerous thing about this type of pronunciation is that
often a reader who has a word like *blesses* or *blesseth* twice in one
verse will often read it *bless-ezz* or *bless-eth* the first time and then
forget and read it *blezz-izz* or *bless-ith* the next time. Usually it is
only the listeners, not the reader, who will be conscious of these
slips. Any kind of unnaturalness is dangerous, because you are
always likely to slip. Of course, if you have no choice but to change
your way of pronouncing a certain pattern of words (that is, if the
dictionary you try to abide by does not allow your way at all), then
you must make the effort to change from an undeniably incorrect
way to a recognized way. But in the case of the suffixes just discussed, you have a choice of accepted pronunciations, and Webster's
certainly says nothing in the Guide to Pronunciation that indicates
that the short e pronunciation is " better " or more literate than the
short i.

Most of us have too great an assignment in eliminating our actual
mistakes to consider trying to change from one accepted pronunciation to another.

SPECIFIC POINTS: PLATFORM MANNER

When you are reading the Bible or any other material in public,
you will observe many of the niceties that you would if you were
making any other kind of appearance on a platform. Naturally you
should not recognize individuals in the audience by smiling, bowing,
or speaking to them or in any other way. A good way to avoid any
possible occasion for this is to keep your eyes just above the heads

of the people in the back row or just below the people in the first row of the balcony. This doesn't mean that you must stare fixedly at one spot; you may look from side to side at various times. Just don't let your eyes keep roving or your head keep turning. And don't gaze at the ceiling or the floor, unless you want to give the impression of being frightened.

Of course, you want to look happy and friendly but don't fix a smile on your face. And don't go to the opposite extreme of looking too solemn. Be dignified but not pompous or austere, pleasant but not informal. *Do's* and *don'ts* are not so helpful as to concentrate on just feeling happy and relaxed and letting it show by acting as natural as possible.

The mouth is a fairly reliable barometer of self-consciousness. Lips held too tight or a fixed smile shows self-consciousness and strain. Some performers in public feel a need of moistening their lips; if this is done too noticeably, it betrays self-consciousness. Sometimes taking two or three deep, slow breaths helps to overcome this feeling.

One sure sign of an inexperienced and self-conscious speaker is a clearing of the throat during or soon after the first word. If you simply must clear your throat, be sure to attend to that as long as possible before you begin to talk or read. If you can do it while your audience is singing, reading, or speaking together, that sound will usually conceal what you are doing.

Another emergency that sometimes arises, especially in the summertime, is having a fly alight on your face. What to do in this uncomfortable situation is a disputed point. Some feel it advisable to read or speak right on, Spartan-fashion, while the fly proceeds wherever he wishes.   Others feel that you should simply brush the fly away, even if this needs to be done more than once; they argue that this course makes your hearers less uncomfortable than watching the fly and wondering how long you will be able to endure the situation.

A similar question arises in regard to what a man should do if he has to seat himself on a platform or stage after the audience has already come into the auditorium. Should he give a slight pull to the knees of his trousers as he sits down or should he sit down without making this homely but natural gesture? Many argue that to make the motion of releasing the strain of the trousers looks uncouth; others say that the men in the audience are all uncomfortable because of thinking of how uncomfortable the one on the platform must be and of worrying about what will happen to the creases in his trousers.

Some public speakers believe that they shouldn't eat a heavy meal just before speaking. Others eat nothing at all. Some eat as much as they wish. It seems to be a matter of individual choice.

Be sure that your clothes are comfortable, correctly arranged, and secure. Assure yourself that everything is perfect before you go out on the platform. It looks amateurish to rearrange part of your clothing or hair-do in front of the audience. Don't wear the kind of dress in which you have to sit or stand one certain way to make it look right or stay right.

Above all, be sure to rehearse in the clothes that you are going to wear. Walk, sit, and stand in them. And have someone observe you.

A noted actress has been quoted as saying, "If you are comfortable on the stage you aren't acting." But she wasn't talking about physical and sartorial comfort. She meant that you must never for a moment relax mentally or take your thoughts off what you are doing. You must be comfortable physically in your clothes and in your attitude of sitting or standing. Never assume an attitude which you think looks nice but which you can't hold comfortably as long as you need to. If an attitude is uncomfortable it is likely to be unnatural and, therefore, wrong.

Be certain that your clothes are appropriate. It should not be necessary to say that they should not be flashy if you are going to read from the Bible or from any other serious or religious book. If you are reading a play whose principal character is a sophisticated woman, don't wear a dress that would be appropriate for grade-school graduation exercises. If the main character is an ingénue, don't wear a slinky black model.

Do not emphasize with your head. Some readers seem unable to stress a word vocally without also jerking their heads downwards. Most people who do this aren't aware of it. As a rule, it is not a good idea to ask advice of friends who have no more technical knowledge of the subject than you have, if as much. Even if they have the perception to sense what is wrong with your reading and think of an improvement, they probably do not know how to express this criticism so that you can understand what they mean. You are likely to be badly misinformed or at least misled and probably will be worse off than before the well-meaning criticism was given. However, if you suspect that one of your faults may be something as simple as head-wagging, you might do well to ask a friend to tell you about this one thing, as anybody can tell you whether your head is moving.

Another solution for the head-wagging mannerism is to practice selections from memory in front of a mirror and watch your head yourself. You may think you are not guilty of this habit and be surprised to learn that you are. If you find it very difficult to break, don't be discouraged. Many others have the same difficulty and it is a habit well worth striving to overcome, because it annoys your audience and focuses attention on you instead of on what you are reading.

Public speakers are sometimes guilty of using meaningless gestures, or too many gestures, of head and arms. Readers are not so often guilty of these bad habits. A radio reader naturally can't depend on using gestures at all for his emphasis, although spontaneous gesturing may make him feel more natural and therefore help him read his lines more naturally; but if his gestures are awkward—and spontaneous ones seldom are—at least his audience doesn't see them. It seems hardly necessary to say that gesturing is entirely out of place in anyone reading aloud from the Bible.

Naturally, a woman should never toy with beads or other jewelry or with a handkerchief, any more than a man should jingle keys or coins in his pockets.

While you are making a speech, if you can't feel comfortable and look natural when letting your arms just hang at your sides, then hold your hands together, put them on the table, or do almost anything with them. It would almost be better to put them into your pockets than to let them hang stiffly. But keep practicing with them hanging. If you continue to hold them in a comfortable position when before an audience and if you practice in private letting them just hang, you will soon begin to feel easy enough to let them hang when you are before an audience.

Other mannerisms that can detract from your reading are habits like playing with a watch fob, raising your eyebrows, holding one shoulder higher than the other, etc. Since the person who does these things is almost unconscious of them, it is a good idea to ask some confidential friend just which habits of this type you are forming.

For the proper way to sit down, rise, stand, and move about on the platform, you will need personal instruction from a good teacher. But the same rules generally apply that apply in a drawing-room: a man waits for a woman to sit first, rises when she rises, etc.

When you sit down or when you rise from a chair, try not to bend forward from the hips. Try to hold yourself straight and erect from the hips up. Another way to put this is, keep your chest in the lead, and don't give the effect of doubling up. To do this smoothly takes some practice. Be careful that you don't jerk yourself up or down and that you don't help yourself up by putting your elbows up and out. When you have risen, move a step or two from your chair so that you will be free of it.

After you rise, wait a moment before you begin to talk or read. Be sure that your hearers are calm and receptive before you begin. (Some speakers call this "subduing your audience.") You can utilize these moments for some deep quiet breathing, also.

SPECIFIC POINTS: READING TECHNIQUE

Announcing the Books of the Bible. There is more to announcing the names of the books of the Bible than you might think. First, don't swallow the name; watch especially the last syllable, as that is the part that is usually slighted. Announce the name clearly and then wait a moment before beginning your reading. Allow your listeners time to hear the name and then time to realize what you have said. While you say " Matthew," your listeners hear " Matthew." While you pause, they think " Matthew.—He's going to read from Matthew."

Don't read the names of the books in a resigned voice. Some readers have a mannerism of reading them almost as a sigh. And don't try to read them with forced " joy." Just announce them in a matter-of-fact, distinct way. If you feel joyful you will sound joyful. If you don't really feel that way about it no amount of "putting" will make your reading sound joyful.

If you are reading from several books of the Bible, be sure to pause after you finish one reading before you announce the book from which you will read next. If you don't make this pause, your hearers won't have time to take in what you have just read before you hurry them on to the next thought. This point is especially important if you are reading on a program with someone else. Don't cut off the previous person's reading with the announcement of the book you will read from. If the previous reader has finished a whole reading, he will have made a point or come to a climax and you do not want to step on it by starting to read or speak before his last word is out. Allow time to count slowly to five before you begin.

There are at least two schools of thought about whether you should look up from your reading, either after you have announced a book of the Bible or while you are reading or after you have finished. Some feel that you should never look up at all. Others say that this procedure is too cold and that you should look up frequently. Still others don't want you to look up too much and yet they like to see you look up after announcing the name of the book of the Bible and perhaps after you have finished reading all the verses from that book. It is certain that looking up takes your hearers' attention from what you are reading and focuses it on you for a moment at least.

Unless you are reading or speaking spontaneously or from memory, you will naturally have your manuscript, book, or books carefully prepared so that you won't have to fumble with hunting pages. If you have to turn a page in the middle of a sentence be sure to put your finger under the page and have it ready to turn. Do this some time before you have to turn it. Nothing sounds much more amateurish than to stop in the middle of a sentence while you struggle to turn a page or find a place. If for any reason you have to look away for a moment, keep your finger on the place.

Inflections. The word *inflection* comes from a Latin word meaning *to bend* and means a bending of the voice. There are four kinds of inflection: straight, rising, falling, and circumflex.

Strictly speaking, a straight inflection is not an inflection at all, since the voice does not bend but remains on the same pitch. Straight inflections are used in singing. Each tone sung on a single pitch is a straight inflection. Straight inflections are seldom used in talking and therefore should seldom be used in reading, as they produce merely a chant or song.

A rising inflection is one in which the voice begins a syllable on one musical tone and then rises to a higher one. Rising inflections are used to denote uncertainty, a questioning attitude, and lack of finality. A direct question that expects an answer of yes or no ends with a rising inflection, as " Are you going? "

A falling inflection is one in which the voice begins a syllable on one musical note and then falls to a lower one. Falling inflections denote finality or a statement, not a question, as in " I am going."

A circumflex inflection means by derivation a " bending around " inflection. It denotes insinuation and, frequently, insincerity. An actor playing an oily, untrustworthy character usually uses many circumflex inflections. Circumflex inflections are sometimes used to flatter or to produce an arch effect, also. In fact, a circumflex inflection is an " arch " of the voice. The voice may begin on a low pitch, rise, and then come down again. Suppose someone said to you something that insinuated a great deal and you replied, " Oh," in a manner that would show you understood the speaker's meaning and perhaps much more. You might raise your eyebrows, shrug your shoulders, and say, " Oh," with a slippery circumflex inflection. It is interesting that the verb *to insinuate* means, by Latin derivation, to move in the manner of a snake, in other words, in curves or arches.

Some readers have a mannerism of using too many rising inflections; some use too many falling. You don't have to wait until the end of a sentence to use a falling inflection. Remember that a rising inflection almost always shows doubt or a question. Try reading Matthew 12:1 with a falling inflection at the end only and see what a peculiar effect it produces. (" At that time Jesus went on the sabbath day through the corn; and his disciples were an hungred, and began to pluck the ears of corn, and to eat.") That is, use rising or straight (level) inflections on *corn, hungred,* and at the second *corn,* and see how meaningless it sounds. Now try slightly dropping your voice at these places and then dropping very definitely on *eat.*

A certain radio comedian gains his comic effects by the clever use of rising inflections where it would be natural to use falling. This simple trick more than his words characterizes him as an ineffectual, prissy flutterbudget.

If you say, " Class, rise," you will use a falling inflection on *rise* or else you will sound as if you are asking a question.

The use of too many falling inflections produces a choppy, disconnected effect. Read Matthew 14:15 with definite falling inflections on *evening, him, saying, place, past, away, villages,* and *victuals.* Now try replacing some of these falling inflections with rising or with less definitely falling inflections and you will see that it sounds more connected and more natural. " And when it was evening, his disciples came to him, saying, This is a desert place, and the time is now past; send the multitude away, that they may go into the villages, and buy themselves victuals."

Inflections are important in the reading of questions. There are two kinds of question. One expects an answer of Yes or No to such as " Are you going? " In conversation we use a rising inflection on this kind of question. We raise not only the inflection but the pitch. There is no reason for doing this; it just comes naturally. But we do have a good reason for using rising inflections when **reading** questions expecting yes-or-no answers: we are trying to read as we talk.

On a question expecting an answer other than Yes or No we naturally use a falling inflection and a falling pitch, as in " Where are you going? "

Matthew 12:11 contains a question that is a little confusing to some readers. " And he said unto them, What man shall there be among you, that shall have one sheep, and if it fall into a pit on the sabbath day, will he not lay hold on it and lift it out? " It is the *he* in the quotation that is misleading, because it makes it sound as if the question were " Will he not lay hold on it, and lift it out? " This expects a yes answer and would call for a rising inflection, which many readers mistakenly use here. But read the whole question (starting with *What*), leaving out the *he* (which is really superfluous, as other translations confirm) and you will see that the question is " What man shall there be . . . that shall have one sheep . . . and will not lay hold on it, and lift it out? " Thus it really expects the answer of " No man" and requires a falling inflection. The question really is not, " Will he lay hold on it, and lift it out? " That would expect a yes answer and would require a rising inflection.

Catalogue Passages. One of the things that readers of the Bible find most difficult to read with freshness and without monotony is the passages that give long lists or repeat the same construction many times. Judicious grouping or phrasing and well-planned inflecting are important in reading these passages.

Romans 8:38 and 39 are considered difficult verses because there is almost no way to vary the reading of the list of ten things. (" For I am persuaded that neither death, nor life, nor angels, nor principalities, nor powers, nor things present, nor things to come, nor height, nor depth, nor any other creature shall be able to separate us from the love of God, which is in Christ Jesus our Lord.") You can try using falling inflections part of the time and rising part of the time. You can try grouping two or three together and then reading one separately. For instance, you might use rising inflections on *death,* on *life,* and perhaps on *angels.* Then you might try a falling on *principalities.* But once you have used a falling, indicating that you are through or almost through, you can't very well go back to rising inflections. You might group *neither death* and *nor life* together, with rising inflection on *death* and falling on *life. Angels, principalities,* and *powers* do not seem to be closely related; so you could read each separately, with a falling inflection. You might couple *things present* with *things to come* and *height* with *depth.* There are numerous other combinations of inflection and grouping that you might make here but all, including the one just suggested, seem like rather obvious attempts to keep the passage from sounding monotonous. Your audience realizes that you are striving to put variety into the reading and perhaps becomes so much absorbed in wondering how you are going to phrase and inflect the next group that it misses some of the meaning. It is probably advisable to read such passages frankly as lists and not struggle to make them sound like anything else.

A verse in which the same construction is repeated is Philippians 4:8: "Finally, brethren, whatsoever things are true, whatsoever things are honest, whatsoever things are just, whatsoever things are pure, whatsoever things are lovely, whatsoever things are of good report; if there be any virtue, and if there be any praise, think on these things." There really isn't much that you can do to keep some of the passages of this type from sounding like anything but lists. But here you might use a circumflex inflection (from high to low to high again) on *true,* rising inflections on *honest* and *just,* and then a falling on *pure.* But once you have used a falling inflection you can hardly go back to a rising without sounding unnatural. Why? Because when you use a rising inflection this signifies that you are expecting to add something to what you have said, that you are not through. If you use a falling, it indicates that you have finished your thought and there is no more to come.

Suppose you use a falling inflection on *pure;* your hearers receive the impression that you have listed all the things you are thinking about (true, honest, just, and pure things). Remember that you are always trying to give the impression that you are just talking, just thinking something through for the first time. You are trying to read this more or less as Paul might have said it when he thought these ideas for the first time. (Now, this does not mean that you are dramatizing it or acting it out, because you are not reading it emotionally, it is to be hoped. You are not using facial expressions or gestures.)

But (your inflections imply) you have another thought, and you add "whatsoever things are lovely." If you use a falling inflection on *lovely,* you will imply that you are through listing things. Then the next thing you mention sounds like another afterthought or spontaneous addition.

On the other hand, so long as you use rising inflections, you imply that you know there is more coming, that you are reading aloud and looking ahead instead of just saying things as you think of them. It is as if you were counting off a long list of things on your fingers: (1) true, (2) honest, (3) just, (4) pure, (5) lovely, (6) of good report. You would be likely to use rising inflections on the first five, when you knew there was more coming, and a falling on the sixth, when you would be finished.

So the use of falling inflections usually conveys more first-time-ness than the use of rising; but to use falling inflections all the way through passages like this can become very monotonous. Perhaps it is better to do that, though, than to struggle for variety. You can hardly keep such passages from sounding monotonous, no matter what you do, and perhaps it is better to read them frankly as lists and let it go at that. Maybe it is more comfortable for your listeners, because they are usually conscious that you are working to produce a natural effect when you begin to use phrasing and inflecting devices on the well-known passages.

Similar problems are found in Psalm 19:7, 8, and 9 and in I Corinthians 12:8, 9, and 10.

But it is a good idea to decide in advance where you will phrase these passages. At least you can avoid grouping together ideas that have no connection. In Mark 10:29 ("And Jesus answered and said, Verily I say unto you, There is no man that hath left house, or brethren, or sisters, or father, or mother, or wife, or children, or lands, for my sake, and the gospel's . . .") there is not much point in trying to make the list sound like anything but a list. But it is startling to hear it read with *sisters* grouped definitely with *father,* for instance, by making pronounced pauses after *brethren* and *father* and no pause at all after *sisters.* If you are going to group, it would certainly be less surprising to group *brethren* with *sisters,* *father* with *mother,* and, perhaps, *wife* with *children.* Sometimes skilful grouping works better than stressing in passages like these.

Relative and Interrogative Who. Sometimes the word *who* is a relative pronoun; sometimes it is an interrogative pronoun. It is interrogative in this sentence: "Who will volunteer to serve?" It is relative in this sentence: "He who hesitates is lost." This *who* refers to its antecedent, *he. He* is the subject of *is lost; who* is the subject of *hesitates. He is lost* is the main clause and *who hesitates* is the subordinate clause.

In earlier English writings, such as the Bible and Shakespeare, and in verse, sometimes the antecedent is unexpressed, as in Iago's famous sentence, " Who steals my purse steals trash." The modern prose form would be: He who steals my purse steals trash.

When you find this relative *who* without its antecedent *he* or *she* (or *I, you, we, they,* etc.) in less familiar sentences than Iago's you must be careful not to make the common mistake of letting it sound like an interrogative. The interrogative is stressed and is pitched rather high; the relative is subdued and low-pitched. Read aloud this sentence: " Who doth a just and righteous deed will always be rewarded." If you fail to subdue the *Who,* you will give your hearers the impression at first that you are asking a question: Who doth a just and righteous deed? Practice reading it with the antecedent expressed: " He who doth a just and righteous deed will always be rewarded." Then try to read the *who* the same way when you leave out the *He.*

The Bible is full of sentences beginning with the relative *who* with its antecedent unexpressed; so it is worth your while to know how to read them so as not to confuse your hearers even momentarily.

Adverb There *and Expletive* There: *Expletive* It; When, Now, etc. The eighth verse of Acts 14 begins: " And there sat a certain man at Lystra . . ." The way you read the second word affects the sense materially. If you stress it, it means " in that place " and it is an adverb. Obviously this is not the meaning. When you subdue it, it becomes an expletive (literally, a " filler " or a " filler-out "), filling or padding the sentence until the meaning-word comes along. The meaning-word in this sentence is *man;* in the more normal order it would read: And a certain man sat at Lystra.

Now, the good reader subdues expletives, but he does not do it arbitrarily simply because he stops to reason: " This word is a mere filler; therefore, it cannot have much meaning; therefore, I shall subdue it." He subdues them because he copies the way we talk and in talking we subdue them without thinking about it, simply because they have no meaning at all.

In the following verse we find an example of the adverb *there:* " And he lighted upon a certain place, and tarried there all night " (Genesis 28:11). You naturally stress this *there,* because it has an important meaning: in that place.

Readers seldom fail to emphasize the adverb *there*. The mistake is in failing to subdue the expletive *there*. This is true especially of readers of the Bible, probably because of the prevalent feeling that it is irreverent not to give full value to every word in the Bible.

In Acts 14:5 we find another expletive *there:* " And when there was an assault made . . ." This passage is a bit difficult to read, since it begins with five " weak " words. *Assault* is the first word with enough meaning to justify emphasis.

Sometimes the word *it* is used as an expletive, as: " It is difficult to explain." (*To explain* is the subject and the more normal form would be: " To explain is difficult.") *It* has no meaning and is not stressed.

There are other words which are seldom emphasized in conversation, such as *when*. Many readers produce an unnatural effect, even though their hearers may not realize what is wrong, by stressing almost every *when*. Perhaps this is accounted for by the fact that *when* is usually near the first of the sentence and many readers, especially of plays and of the Bible, tend to start each sentence on a high pitch and come down. (Maybe you do; test yourself.) This produces an overly-cheerful effect. In natural conversation *when* is not stressed except for some definite reason, such as contrast. If you said, " When he arrives, we shall be very happy," you would not stress *when*. But, if you said, " I didn't ask whether he was coming; I asked when he was coming," you would stress *when* in contrast with *whether*.

Sometimes the Bible uses the word *one* where we today would say *someone,* as in Jeremiah 10:3: " For the customs of the people are vain: for one cutteth a tree out of the forest, the work of the hands of the workman, with the axe." If it is read with even a little emphasis on *one,* it makes it sound as if it implied a contrast with several people, or as if one cutteth a tree and another doeth something else. If you practice it with *someone* instead of *one,* you will see that the *one* receives no emphasis. It is a bit difficult to read it as it stands without emphasizing *one* but with practice it can be done and the added sense and naturalness it gives the passage is worth the practice.

The word *now* does not always mean *at this time*. Often it has almost no meaning, as in Ezra 4:14: "Now because we have maintenance from the king's palace, and it was not meet for us to see the king's dishonour, therefore have we sent and certified the king." To emphasize *now* in a context like this throws the listener off for a moment, causing him to think that it means *at this time,* when in reality it is merely an introductory word with almost no significance.

Participial Construction. A participle is partly adjective and partly verb. In Psalm 49:12 we read: "Nevertheless man being in honour abideth not . . ." *Being* is a part of the verb *to be;* it is also an adjective, because it modifies the noun, *man.*

In Luke 3:21 we read: "Now . . . Jesus also being baptized, and praying, the heaven was opened." *Being baptized* is a participle and *praying* is a participle, from the verbs *to baptize* and *to pray,* respectively. But instead of merely modifying the noun *Jesus,* they are used as verbs or predicates of *Jesus. Jesus being baptized, and praying* is equal to a clause with subject and verb: when Jesus was baptized and prayed. This is called an absolute construction. In this verse it is logical not to pause between the subject and its predicate, as there are already several necessary pauses in this rather complicated verse. Also, if you do pause after *Jesus,* you lead your listeners for a moment to think that *being baptized* and *praying* are modifying *Jesus* instead of making the actual statements about what Jesus did. So they will expect to hear a further statement made about Jesus. But the main statement or clause in this sentence is about *the heaven:* "the heaven was opened."

In the verse from Psalms quoted two paragraphs above, we have a different construction. *Being* modifies *man;* it is not the predicate of *man.* It describes man but does not make a statement about what man does or is. *Abideth* is the word that does that; *abideth* is a verb, the predicate of *man.* In this case you must be careful to see that you do pause before the participle or your listeners will think for a short while that *being* is all you are going to say about *man,* when you are really about to say that man abideth not. If you give the impression that *man* is the subject of *being,* you will not have any subject left for *abideth.*

Of course, the listener probably will not put these misapprehensions into words mentally. He wouldn't have time to even if he

were able to, as many listeners don't know a participle from a preposition. The misunderstanding will last for only a moment but the
listeners nevertheless will receive a misleading impression. And such
reading is distracting. Listening to it is like trying to extract the
meaning from an illegibly written letter. Usually it can be done but
it is unsatisfactory. And the effect of such reading on listeners who
really know good reading from bad and who know the reasons for
both is positively painful. Never underestimate your audience. Dis-
criminating listeners are more numerous than most people think and
are increasing in number.

Even audiences that know little about grammar or technique
appreciate clear reading, even though they may not realize how the
reader achieves clarity. Only an experienced cook can tell merely
by tasting a cake what ingredients were used and what was wrong
with the method, but a person who knows nothing at all about
cooking can tell whether it tastes good. A listener can usually figure
out of the meaning of a reader who does not know how to give the
sense, just as a diner can add salt to the dish after it is cooked and
served. But it is better to have it seasoned in advance by the cook.

Because that, etc. There are several constructions used in the
King James translation of the Bible which employ short words that
are not used in the same way in modern English: such expressions
as " what and if " where we today say " what if," " after that "
where we say " after," and " because that" where we say
" because."

In John 6:62 we find: " What and if ye shall see the Son of man
ascend up where he was before? " The most nearly natural way to
read this is just to subdue the *and*.

Hebrews 10:2 says, in part, ". . . because that the worshippers
once purged should have had no more conscience of sins." It is easy
to subdue *that* and make the sense clear.

Mark 14:28 reads: " But after that I am risen, I will go before
you into Galilee." As it means simply " after I am risen," all you
need to do is to subdue *that*. Failure to subdue *that* in this particular
instance, especially if you also pause after *that,* changes the meaning
considerably.

Mixture of Direct and Indirect Quotation. Once in a while you will find a Bible verse in which there is a quotation which is neither direct nor indirect or which might be said to be both direct and indirect. Luke 7:16 reads: " And there came a fear on all: and they glorified God, saying, That a great prophet is risen up among us; and, That God hath visited his people." If it were purely direct quotation it might read: And they glorified God, saying, " A great prophet is risen up among us and God hath visited his people." But if it were purely indirect quotation the wording might be the same except that the pronouns and the tenses of the verbs would change: And they glorified God, saying that a great prophet was risen up among them and God had visited his people.

If they were written as purely direct quotations, you would probably pause before the beginning of the quotation. If they were purely indirect, you probably would not pause before *that,* which introduces the indirect quotation. As it is actually written, it is probably advisable not to pause between *saying* and *That,* even though they are separated by a comma and even though *That* begins with a capital.

Articulation. Many passages in the Bible present difficulties in articulation, that is, enunciation. To read the Bible clearly you must watch your *d's* and *t's.*

T and *d* are made with the tip of the tongue at the top of the upper teeth. The difference between them is simply that *d* is voiced and *t* is voiceless. You can prove this by putting your finger on your larynx and saying the sound of *t* and then the sound of *d*. (The larynx is what is commonly called the Adam's apple and is commonly mispronounced as if it were spelled larnyx, with the first syllable rhyming with *bar* or, sometimes, with *bear,* and the second syllable rhyming with *mix;* but the word is actually lar-ynx, the first syllable rhyming more or less with *bear* and the second with *thinks.*) When you put your finger on your larynx, do not say the name of the letters *t* and *d;* say just the sounds of the letters— *t-t-t* and *d-d-d.* When you say the sound of *t* (not tee), you will feel no vibration in your larynx. When you say the sound of *d* (not dee), you will feel vibration. This vibration is due to the fact that you are actually humming or using your voice when you say the sound of *d* but you are simply letting air escape without any voice when you say the sound of *t*.

In verbs ending with the sound of *k, p, f, ch,* or *sh,* when you add *-ed* to form the past tense, the *-ed* is pronounced like a *t* and does not add a syllable. *Looked* is lookt; *tapped,* tapt; *sniffed* and *laughed,* snift and laft; *lashed,* lasht; and *latched,* latcht.

Words like *risked* and *asked,* which end in the sounds -skt, are hard to articulate. The word *asked* occurs often in the Bible and warrants much practice. Almost anybody can say *ask* but when it changes to *asked* (askt) many people solve the difficulty by calling it simply *ast* or even *ask,* because they find it difficult to articulate the *k* between the *s* and the *t*. Remember that *t* is simply a voiceless lifting of the tip of the tongue to the top of the upper teeth. Say *ask* and then quickly lift your tongue to your upper teeth and pop it away from them.

Be careful not to say *aska-t.* Don't make an extra syllable of the *k.* That is just as bad as leaving it out altogether and saying *ast.*

Try the same thing with *risked.* Make a little exercise: ris—risk—riskt.

A similar difficulty arises in saying *Acts.* It is *akts.* Many find it so hard to sound the *t* between the *k* and the *s* that they call it simply *Axe—aks,* without sounding the *t* at all. Practice ak—akt—akts. Again, be careful not to make a separate syllable of the *t.* Don't call it *Akta-ss.*

Practice a word like *tests,* ending in -sts. Many people, instead of saying "One test—two tests," say merely "One test—two tess." In other words, instead of adding an *s* to form the plural, they simply drop the *t!* Practice tes—test—tests, remembering just to raise your tongue for a split second. You are making an *s* sound, you silently raise your tongue to the *t* position, and then you drop it right back to the *s* position. It will automatically give the effect of pronouncing *t.* Again, be careful not to say *testa-ss.*

If you can say *tests,* you are ready to try a more complicated word like *texts.* There is still another sound to produce here. *Texts* ends in -ksts. (You make a *k* by raising the back of your tongue against the velum. The velum is the soft part between the hard roof of the mouth and what is commonly miscalled the soft palate but is really the uvula.) Practice tek—teks—tekst—teksts. The difficult part will be to be sure to raise your tongue to form the *t* sound without making an extra syllable.

Don't fail to sound final *t's*. To omit them is to leave off part of your word, like leaving off the right side of a picture frame. To stress final *t's* too heavily is like using too large and heavy a frame.

Psalm 138:3 and Nehemiah 1:7-11 are excellent verses to practice. In fact, they almost have to be practiced if they are read smoothly. *Answeredst* and *strengthenedst* are simply *answer* and *strengthen* with *-edst* added as an extra syllable. Many people agree that it sounds more natural to pronounce *-edst* with a short *i* instead of short *e*. It is only one syllable formed of four sounds: *-idst*. It is not *-ed-est* or *-id-ist,* with two extra syllables added to the word. Don't try to hurry yourself in pronouncing such words.

Didst is pronounced just as it is spelled, with five sounds. *Shewest* is two syllables, just as spelled; it is *shew* plus *-est*. If it were spelled *shew'st,* it would be pronounced in one syllable, just as spelled. You can always depend on that. If it is spelled *givest* or *diddest,* it has two syllables. *Did'st* or *giv'st* would have just one.

The words *hast asked* occur together in II Chronicles 1:11, making a difficult trap for a reader. Just practice the two words thoroughly and then proceed deliberately when reading the verse. Don't practice as you read. Do all your practicing first and then read deliberately, after planning numerous places to pause, and don't let yourself become excited about it.

When you know a word is coming up that is difficult to pronounce or articulate, don't read right up to the word and then stop. You might as well announce to your listeners that you have come to a difficult word and will have to stop and practice silently a moment before you attempt it. The thing to do is to decide on the nearest place where you can logically pause, even marking it if necessary; then stop on that pausing place, make sure that you can say the difficult word, and then go on and read the whole phrase containing it.

Final and internal *d's* are important, too. The *d* in *commandment* is frequently not sounded, although of course it should be. *Comman'ment* sounds careless. But be careful not to put in an extra syllable and make *commandament*. Just raise your tongue for a moment to make the *d*.

In Colossians 3:2 are the words: " Set your affection . . ." A *t* sound before a *y* sound will run into a *ch* sound if you aren't careful. Don't let it be: Setchoor affection.

" Except ye see signs . . . " (John 4:48) should not become *Exceptchee see signs.* Always keep a *t* and a *y* separate—but don't strain over it.

A *d* sound and a *y* sound become fused in a *j* sound unless you are careful. Don't let *did you* and *could you* merge into *didjoo* and *couldjoo.*

More about Carry-over. " So they read in the book in the law of God distinctly, and gave the sense, and caused them to understand the reading " (Nehemiah 8:8).

One of the most important things to remember in oral reading of the Bible is that you are not just feeding out words. You are giving out ideas. Furthermore, the ideas carry over from one verse to the next, sometimes even from one chapter to the next. However, many readers fail to see or to bring out this carry-over of ideas, even from one phrase to the next within the same sentence. For a detailed discussion of this important point, see Chapter II, concerning Carry-over; Different Meaning at Different Times. Please do not continue reading this chapter until you have read or reread the section just mentioned.

After you have done so, you will be ready to consider the subject of carrying over the connection in a passage like Matthew 23:9. " And call no man your father upon the earth: for one is your Father, which is in heaven." Often it is read or quoted alone, in which case both *father* and *earth* are new ideas, to be stressed. But now precede it with the seventh and eighth verses: " And greetings in the markets, and to be called of men, Rabbi, Rabbi. But be not ye called Rabbi: for one is your Master, even Christ; and all ye are brethren." *Call* becomes an old idea, and doesn't *earth* become an implied old idea? And isn't *father* both a new idea and a contrast with *Rabbi* or *Master?* Therefore, shouldn't *father* be the only word emphasized of the first nine words in the ninth verse?

Most Bible verses are complete sentences and, therefore, whole ideas; so we usually stop at the end of each Bible verse. But sometimes a verse ends in the middle of a thought and naturally we should keep right on going just as though the two verses were written without a break. Usually there should be no pause, or only a short pause, between the verses, and usually you should keep your inflection up at the end of the first verse, although this is not always necessary.

Instances of connected verses in the Bible are so numerous that it is hardly necessary to list any, but, since some readers always stop at the end of a Bible verse as unfailingly as others stop at the end of a line of poetry, it seems advisable to call attention to the following verses: Psalm 96:12 and 13 constitutes an outstanding instance of a place where you should make no pause at all and give no downward inflection between verses.

Miscellaneous Special Constructions. There are a number of special Biblical constructions which a reader should know how to handle. The translators of the King James version often used the word *that* differently from the way we do today. In Romans 6:10 we read: "For in that he died, he died unto sin once." We use this expression *in that* today, to mean inasmuchas or insofaras and we subdue the *that*.

But in Matthew 27:31 we find the expression *after that,* in a construction not usual today: "And after that they had mocked him, they took the robe from off him." Some readers actually stress *that* and pause before the first *they,* as though *that* were the object of *after*. This reading makes "And after that—they had mocked him" sound like a complete though meaningless sentence; but the fact that it is followed by a comma instead of a period shows that it is not. This type of construction is simple when you realize that the *that* in *after that* would be left out in modern speaking. All it means is *after*. So, since you certainly can't think of leaving out *that* in your reading, you have to subdue the *that* in such constructions. It means merely: and after they had mocked him.

Naturally, every *after that* in the Bible does not mean simply *after*. In John 11:7, the *that* is really the object of *after* and the verse should be read with some stress on *that* and with a pause before *saith.* "Then after that saith he to his disciples, Let us go into Judaea again."

The King James version uses *because that* where we would now say *because.* In Hebrews 10:2 we read: ". . . because that the worshippers once purged should have had no more conscience of sins." All we can do is to subdue the *that.*

II Corinthians 5:4 reads: "For we that are in this tabernacle do groan, being burdened: not for that we would be unclothed, but clothed upon, that mortality might be swallowed up of life." The expression *for that* would be, in modern English, *that* but we would not stress the *that.* So we would read this verse with both *for* and *that* subdued.

An odd usage that confuses some readers occurs in Luke 13:25. "When once the master of the house is risen up, and hath shut to the door, and ye begin to stand without . . ." The *to* after *hath shut* is often subdued; but since the expression seems to mean "hath shut the door to," isn't it sensible to stress *to,* even though it precedes *the door* instead of following it? It helps here not to pause before *to* and perhaps to make a very slight pause after *to.*

Similarly the *and* should be subdued in the expression *but and if* in Matthew 24:48. "But and if that evil servant shall say in his heart . . ."

If the passage you are reading contains unfamiliar words or words that are no longer a part of our language, as is often the case in Shakespeare or the Bible, substitute familiar and modern words that mean the same thing and practice reading the passage with these substitutions. Remember, for instance, in reading the Bible that *divers* means simply diverse, or different, and that *severally* means separately. Practice reading in this way verses like I Corinthians 12:11 ("But all these worketh that one and the selfsame Spirit, dividing to every man severally as he will") and Luke 4:40 ("Now when the sun was setting, all they that had any sick with divers diseases brought them unto him"). Sometimes people stress *divers* instead of *diseases,* since *divers* looks like a strange and rather impressive word. But if you will only remember that the phrase means "diverse diseases" or "different diseases," you will naturally stress *diseases* in this and every such passage. The obsolete meaning of *several* was *separate, distinct, apart.* Substitute these meanings here and in the Shakespearean quotation beginning with "my conscience" on Page 25.

In the numerous instances where a direct quotation is preceded by the words "Verily, verily," readers often read these two words as a meaningless formula: verily-verily. But remember that the actual meaning of the word *verily* is *truly.* Now practice reading one of these passages and substituting *truly* for *verily.* You will probably pause after the first *truly* and stress the second, as the reason for repeating it must have been for emphasis. "Verily, verily, I say unto you, He that believeth on me, the works that I do shall he do also" (John 14:12).

More about Quotations. Be sure to pause long enough after a direct quotation to let your hearers know that it is ended, or they may think that the next thing you read is part of the quotation. In reading modern writings this difficulty can be avoided by saying, "End of quotation." But naturally this device cannot be used when you are reading from the Bible; the skill of the reader must prevent misunderstanding. In John 4:53 we read: "So the father knew that it was at the same hour, in the which Jesus said unto him, Thy son liveth: and himself believed, and his whole house." The whole quotation is "Thy son liveth." But, unless you stop for a pause after *liveth,* it could sound as if he had said, "Thy son liveth and himself believed and his whole house." A little thought, of course, would show that the whole thing is not part of the quotation; but by the time your listeners have stopped to figure this out, they may have missed hearing the next verse. Besides, you are supposed to thresh out possibilities ahead of time for your listeners; they are not supposed to have to do it for themselves.

"For many shall come in my name, saying, I am Christ; and shall deceive many" (Matthew 24:5). The "many" are quoted as saying nothing but "I am Christ"; but, unless you pause unmistakably after these three words, it will sound as if they are to say, "I am Christ and shall deceive many."

This same pitfall should be guarded against in II Kings 5:12, and in John 4:50, and in any other verse where you have a quotation from a conversation followed immediately by a continuation of the narrative.

Some Puzzling Diacritical Markings. Diacritical markings are symbols used to indicate the sounds of vowels and consonants and to indicate the accents in recording the pronunciations of words. Some people find them difficult to urderstand and so this book includes short explanations of a few of Webster's diacritical markings. Most of the simple long and short vowels are generally understood but some of the others puzzle people.

When people look up words like *Pharaoh* and *Mary,* they notice that the a in *Mary* and the first a in *Pharaoh* are now marked with a circumflex symbol: â. They then look at the key word at the bottom of the page, which is *care.* Since most people use a pure short a (as in *add*) in *care,* they immediately think that circumflex a in *care* sounds just like short a in *add* and that they must, therefore, pronounce *Mary* just like *marry.* This is not the case.

The explanation is that the circumflex a is a sound somewhere between long a as in *ale* and short e as in *end.* Few people use it in *care.* As Webster's dictionary notes a range of sounds for circumflex a, it would be difficult to say that it is actually wrong to sound it as short a when it occurs in *Mary, Pharaoh, dairy, various,* etc., but certainly you don't **have** to pronounce *Mary* as *marry,* etc. And, if you don't pronounce *Mary as May-ry* naturally, you needn't struggle to do so. To sound it just between *May-ry* and *Merry* is a true circumflex a.

Nature is Webster's key word for tū. This sound may be either tyoo or choo; it is either na-tyoor or na-cher, fu-tyoor or fu-cher, over-tyoor or over-choor. Many, if not most, people feel that the na-tyoor and fu-tyoor style sounds affected and stilted. It is certainly unnatural to almost everyone, although many of the people who say na-cher and fu-cher use the other style naturally in words like over-tyoor and litera-tyoor. It may be all right to mix them in informal speaking but perhaps it is advisable to stick to one pronunciation or the other if you are speaking or reading in public. Probably the na-cher-and-over-choor pronunciation will please more people. The point is that the tū marking does not force you to say na-tyoor, etc.

The marking dū is similar, the key word being *verdure.* This has the formal pronunciation dyoo and the informal joo. Some people feel that edjoocate is a careless pronunciation of *educate;* others feel that edyoocate is stilted. Probably those who approve of edjoocate are more numerous. Other words in which this sound occurs are *individual, modulate, pendulum,* etc. The point is that the marking du͝ does not force you to say verdyoor, etc.

Most words that Webster's formerly marked with a long e followed by an r now are marked with ẹ. *Here,* once marked hēr, is now hẹr. This means that the r following the long e reduces it to what is virtually a short i sound (as in *ill*). So you do not have to struggle to say cee-real or matee-rial. Short i sound (marked as ẹ) is allowable instead of the full long e.

Understanding diacritical markings requires a sharp eye for detail. Be careful to distinguish between ă, à, ĕ, ĭ, ŏ, ŭ on the one hand and *ă, à ĕ, ĭ, ŏ, ŭ* on the other. In the first group ă, ĕ, ĭ, ŏ, and ŭ are full short vowels as in *add, end, ill, odd,* and *up,* respectively; à is short Italian a as in *ask,* between short a and broad, or long Italian, a. In the second group the primary sound of each is the same, an obscure vowel, like *uh* without any accent, as in *account, sofa, silent, charity, connect,* and *circus,* respectively. The only difference in the markings, despite the great difference in the sounds of the various pairs, is that in the first set the vowels are printed in roman and in the second they are italicized. The markings above them are the same. This is a point often overlooked.

Another detail to watch is the accents. A student of these markings once puzzled a long time over Webster's pronunciation of *irreconcilable.* Finally the student gave it up and concluded that the dictionary had made a mistake and written the same pronunciation twice. The vowels were all marked exactly alike and the accents were like this: ĭr-rĕk'-ŏn-sĭl'-à-b'l; ĭr-rĕk'-ŏn-sĭl'-à-b'l. He hadn't looked closely enough to see that, in the first pronunciation, the second syllable had a light accent and the fourth a heavy. In the second pronunciation the light and heavy accents were reversed. That was the only difference in the two pronunciations.

Biblical Words Often Mispronounced. Many experienced readers agree that it is the words you know how to pronounce that trip you. The long words that you know you can't pronounce you will look up, but the little words that you think you know are the ones you don't look up, and they are the ones that trick you.

One of the shortest words is also one of the most often mispronounced: the three-letter, one-syllable word, *and*. Almost everyone pronounces it correctly in conversation, but hand him a script or a book and he is more than likely to give it a stilted broad a: *ahnd*.

Now whether you say *can't* (à as in *ask*) or *cahn't* is beside the point. *Can't* is good American; *cahn't* is good British (and American in some places). But *ahnd* isn't good anything. Neither Webster, an American authority, nor Daniel Jones,* a British authority, lists *ahnd*.

Webster gives three pronunciations of *and*. If you stress it, you use a full short a, and it rhymes with *band*. You would use this pronunciation in reading the second verse of the first chapter of Genesis: "And the earth was without form." Webster lists also two unstressed forms, approximately *'nd* and *'n'*. You might use the second unstressed pronunciation in saying "Adam 'n' Eve" very informally. You would never use it in formal reading or speaking. The form *'nd* is frequently and appropriately used in formal as well as informal reading. To use the stressed form every time would sound unnatural.

The British dictionary mentioned gives all these forms and gives in addition two more unstressed forms: *'m* and *'ng*. In case you are wondering when you might pronounce *and* as *'m* or *'ng*, try saying " top and bottom " and " lock and key " quickly and they may sound like " top 'm bottom " and " lock 'ng key."

About the only pronunciation not allowed, indeed, is *ahnd*. *Ahnd* is not natural to anybody, as is proved by the fact that almost everyone that tries to use it sometimes forgets and rhymes *and* with *band*.

The article a is never pronounced like a long a (to rhyme with *bay*) unless you want to stress it, as in saying, " Not several boys but just a boy." Unstressed, as it usually is, it is simply an obscure vowel, like the first syllable of *above*. *An* is pronounced with a short

---

* *An English Pronouncing Dictionary* by Daniel Jones. Copyright 1937, 1946, by E. P. Dutton & Co., Inc., New York.

a (to rhyme with *ran*) only when stressed. Unstressed it always has an obscure vowel and sounds like the first two sounds in *anew*.

The article *the* has a long e (like *thee*) only when stressed or placed before vowel sounds, as *the apple* (thee) apple or "not just any Mr. Shaw but the (thee) Mr. Shaw." Unstressed and before consonants it has only an obscure vowel sound and amounts to something like *th' banana*.

What is another monosyllable that gives trouble. Rhyming it with *hut* is a careless pronunciation. It should rhyme with *hot*. Practice: What a hot pot! *Saith* has only one syllable. It means say-eth but is not pronounced that any more than *said* is pronounced say-ed. *Saith* should sound like *Seth*. *Shew* is pronounced *show*. *Sloth* rhymes with either *both* or *broth*. *Err* is a peculiar word, in that it rhymes with *blur* and has that sound of the vowel in all forms except *erring*, which has a choice of two vowel sounds. *Erring* may rhyme with either *blurring* or *herring*.

The first syllable of *comely* and of *compass* rhymes with *sum*. It does not rhyme with either *comb* or *Tom*.

Sinew is sometimes mispronounced as *sin-oo* and *Matthew* as *Math-oo*. They should be *sin-yoo* and *Math-yoo*.

The first syllable of *ravening* rhymes with *have*. It does not rhyme with *brave*.

The second syllable of *sincerity* does not sound as it does in *sincere*. *Sincerity* rhymes with *verity*.

Some readers try to be too particular with *generation*. They sound the second e long. This is wrong. The first two syllables of *generation* do not sound like *Jenny*. They are like the first two syllables of *general*.

Resurrection, too, is often given too fancy a pronunciation, with the second syllable pronounced as yoo. The first two syllables should be pronounced like the first two in *reservoir*.

The last syllables of *infidel* and *citadel* do not rhyme with *bell*. They sound clipped like the last syllable of *cradle*.

Don't rhyme the last syllable of *Gilead* with *bad*. It is clipped, with an obscure vowel, more like the last syllable of *myriad*.

Throughly should not sound like *thoroughly*. It is pronounced as it is spelled, to rhyme with *truly*.

Sometimes people try to pronounce *woman* just as it is spelled, to rhyme with *Roman,* but the first two letters should sound like the first two letters in *wolf* not in *woke.* And *women* rhymes with *swimmin'.*

The last syllable of *yesterday* may have either short i or long a. Be careful not to let the d in *midst* become a t. It is *midst,* not *mitst.*

Triumph is simply *triumf.* It is not *triumth. Triumphing* is *trium-fing,* not *trium-thing* nor *triumf-thing.*

The " sitting-down " pronunciation of *sacrifice* (the noun) has a long i in the last syllable, making it rhyme with *price.* But the " standing-up " pronunciation almost invariably has a short i in the last syllable, rhyming it with *miss.* That is, many or even most people use the long i in conversation but, whenever they come across the word in something they are reading before an audience, they feel obliged to give it a more dressed-up pronunciation and use the short i. Until a very recent edition of Webster's, the short i was not allowed at all. The last syllable had long i only and could rhyme with either *price* or *prize.* Now, however, Webster lists the short i, also.

Nevertheless, many careful speakers are inclined to go on using the pronunciations which have long been approved and to shun those which have not been allowed until recently. If this attitude seems snobbish, it has a practical value which should not be ignored. If you are speaking before a group that is inclined to be critical of pronunciation, it is a good idea to stay with the long-approved pronunciations, if they are still allowed. This seems especially advisable when you consider that many of your listeners, even the very careful ones, will be unaware that the formerly " incorrect " pronunciation has been accepted in the very latest edition of whatever dictionary you use. Therefore, many speakers feel it desirable still not to use a short i in the last syllable of *sacrifice.*

The same thing is true of three other words which all but the most careful speakers have mispronounced for years: *traverse, thither,* and *thence. Traverse* is usually accented on the second syllable although Webster's has for years accented the first syllable, with no choice. Only recently has Webster allowed both ways of accenting it. But informed listeners, hearing you stress the second syllable, would probably think you were making a mistake. Those few even better informed listeners who have checked it with the very latest edition might think that you had not done so but were just using an old mispronunciation. Until recently, the sound of each th in *thither* and *thence* had to be like the th in *then*. The th in *thin* was not allowed. But recently Webster's has included the sound of th in *thin* for the one in *thence* and for the first th in *thither*. The old pronunciations are still allowed, however, and here again many speakers who have trained themselves to use them still prefer them.

Heaven, seven, eleven, devil, and *evil* are sometimes given a short i sound in the last syllable: *hevinn, sevinn, elevinn, devill,* and *evill*. In some of them Webster's shows the short i; in some it is not shown. Many people feel that short i in these words is unnatural and stilted and they prefer the plainer *heav'n, sev'n,* etc.

Accent is the problem with many words. *Mundane, travail,* and *chastisement* are accented on the first syllable. (And the i in *chastisement* is short.) *Travail* is probably one of the most frequently mispronounced words in the Bible. The second syllable may have a long a but no accent. Or *travail* may be pronounced just like *travel*. It seems a good idea, though, not to use the latter choice, since it would not only surprise many listeners but confuse them. English has so many words that must be pronounced alike that when you can make a distinction between two words of similar pronunciation, it is a good thing to do so, for the sake of clearness. In pronunciation, as in phrasing and emphasizing, it is better not to use an unusual choice merely for the sake of being spectacular. It takes your hearers' attention for a moment at least from what you say next.

The noun *torment* is accented on the first syllable; the verb, on the second.

Blaspheme and *baptize* are accented on the second syllable. And be sure to pronounce it *baptize* and not *babtize*. The opposite substitution (of the p for the b sound) is incorrectly made in *Jacob*. It is *Jacob,* not *Jacup*.

Applicable should be accented on the first syllable and *inexplicable* on the second.

Peniel has two permissible pronunciations. It may rhyme with *denial* or with *centennial.*

The first syllable of *authority* is *awe,* not *uh,* like the first syllable of *author.*

The first pronunciation Webster's gives for *Jairus* is with the accent on the first syllable, clipping the second syllable. (Clipping means pronouncing very quickly, usually with only an obscure vowel; it does not mean leaving out.) This makes a pronunciation that rhymes almost exactly with *mayoress.* But many people find this pronunciation exceedingly difficult, as they tend to put the r in the wrong place. If you find yourself saying Ja'-ri-us (like *dairy-us*) instead of *Ja'i-rus* (like *mayoress* or *player-us*), it would be sensible just to use Webster's other pronunciation, with the i long and accented, making it rhyme with *May-Cyrus.* Whenever you find that you simply can't use one pronunciation without tripping, even though that pronunciation is decidedly preferred, common sense says to use an easier one, if there is one allowable at all.

Don't put extra letters into words. *Grievous* has only two syllables. There is no i after the v. It is *griev-us* (like *leave-us*), not *griev-i-us,* like *devious.* There is no i after the v in *mischievous.* It is not *mis-cheev-i-us* (like *devious*). The first syllable is accented and the second is clipped instead of having an accented long e.

Don't pronounce *height* as if it had an h after the t. Because of the th at the end of *length, depth, width,* and *breadth,* there is a tendency to add the same sound to *height.* Formerly *height* was spelled with an h at the end and was pronounced accordingly; but for a long time that spelling and pronunciation have not been considered good usage. *Height* rhymes with *kite.*

Sometimes even the letters that are actually there are not all to be pronounced. The l in *Psalms* should not be sounded. *Psalms* rhymes with *palms.*

Seldom does anyone sound all the letters that should be sounded in *clothes.* It usually is pronounced like the verb *close,* to rhyme with *rose,* but the th should be sounded, followed by the z sound of the s. This is hard for some people to articulate. Instead of going directly from the long o to the z sound, put your tongue between your teeth to make the sound of th in *then*. Then make the z sound.

Sometimes the pronunciation of one word is confused with that of a similar word. The second syllable of *beneficent* is accented and should sound like *neff*, not *niff*. But it is often mispronounced *niff* because of confusion with *magnificent*, a more familiar word.

Many people pronounce *portentous* as if it had an i after the t. It is not *portentious* (*por-ten-shus*); it is *portent-us*, like *momentous*. It is just the word *portent*, with the second syllable accented and *-ous* added. Why is it so generally mispronounced? Because we are more familiar with *pretentious*, which does have an i after the t.

Terrestrial should be pronounced just as spelled. But, because *celestial* is a word we use more often, people overlook the r after the second t in *terrestrial* and rhyme it with *celestial*. But *terrestrial* has four syllables, not just three. It is *ter-res-tri-al*, not *ter-res-chul*.

Reverend ends with a d sound, unlike *reverent*, which ends in t. *Iron* is not *i-ron* but *i-ern*.

Sometimes *malefactor* is given only three syllables, with a long a in the first: *male-fac-ter*. But it has four and the a is short: *mal-e-fac-ter*.

In *leasing*, as used in the Bible to mean *lying*, the " s " has the sound of z not s.

Speakers sometimes think they must strive to put four syllables into *Colossians* but Webster's shows only three: *Co-losh-ans*. Probably because *Ephesus* starts with a short e, people sometimes take pains to start *Ephesians* with a short e. But it starts with the equivalent of a long e.

Zion starts with a z sound; *Sion*, with an s.

If you are British, you will naturally use British pronunciations and a British dictionary. But if you are American, you will be sensible to confine yourself to American pronunciation and use an American dictionary, such as Webster's *New International*, which is the authority for the pronunciations explained here. There are two recognized standards of pronunciation, American and British, and one is just as " good " as the other. Most Americans require much work to improve their use of American diction and if anyone tries to superimpose imitation British diction over American local speech patterns (whether Midwestern, Eastern, Southern, Brooklyn, or what) he is almost certain to achieve a ridiculous effect.

One of the numerous ways to detect an imitation British accent is the pronunciation of the word *fancy*. Often a person who has trained himself to say *cahn't, ahfter,* etc., when broad a's are not natural to him, will use a broad a in *fancy,* too. This proves his British accent to be synthetic, as even the British use short a in *fancy*. The first syllable rhymes with *man*.

The American pronunciation of *circumstance* rhymes the last syllable with *prance*. Clipping it to *circumst'nce* is more British. On the other hand, *trespass* should have the last syllable clipped: *tres-p'ss*. The second syllable of *steadfast* may be given full value (*stead-fast*) or may be clipped to *stead-f'st*.

The pronunciation of *Luke* is usually troublesome. Long u (as in *cube*) usually should be *yoo,* not just *oo*. Most people naturally pronounce it as *yoo* when it follows the sounds of b, c or k, f, g, h, m, p, and v, as in *butane, cube* or *kudize, fuse, legume, huge, music, puny,* and *revue*. (Nobody says *hooge, moosic, revoo,* etc.) But many give it the *oo* sound when it follows the sounds of d, t, and n, as in *duke, Tuesday,* and *news,* respectively. They call them *dook, Toozday,* and *nooz* instead of *dyook, Tyoozday,* and *nyooz*. Very few pronounce it as *yoo* when it follows the sounds of l, s, z, and th, as in *Luke, suit, resume* or *exuberant,* and *enthusiasm,* respectively. Few people naturally say *Lyook, syoot, rezyoom, egzyooberant,* and *enthyoosiasm*. Almost everyone, unless he has trained himself, says *Look, soot, rezoom, egzooberant,* and *enthoosiasm*.

Now Webster's does not say you have to say *Lyook* or *dyook*. But, after a careful study of Webster's discussion of the long u and careful listening to recognized speakers, you may arrive at this conclusion: (1) Nobody needs to bother about the first classification (*butane,* etc.), since we all give it the *yoo* sound naturally. (2) It is highly desirable to train yourself to say *yoo* in the second group (*duke,* etc.) if you don't do so anyway. (3) Many feel that the *yoo* sound in the third group (*Luke,* etc.) sounds affected; some think that even though it may sound a bit uncustomary at first it should be used, at least in formal speaking and reading.

So you may conclude that it is really advisable to train yourself (or have a good teacher train you) to use the *yoo* sound following d, t, and n sounds. It is easy to learn. Even though you may not always be consistent with it at first in conversation, you can start using it in reading, if you have your material ahead of time and can mark the words and practice them. But, if you must read your material, such as radio scripts, at sight, you would do better to practice until you are consistent with the sounds in conversation before you try them before seen or unseen audiences.

But the *Luke* group presents a practical hazard. To say *Lyook* smoothly is difficult for some speakers. It is better just to say *Lōok* than to stumble over *Lyook*. *Suit* is still more difficult, because, unless you are very careful, *syoot* becomes *shoot*. It is lovely to be able to say nonchalantly, " I have a blue *syoot* " but it is better to say, " I have a blue *soot* " than " I have a blue *shoot*." Also, if you do start saying *Lyook*, to be consistent you should use the *yoo* sound after s, z, and th sounds, too. So don't start on *Lyook* unless you can toss off words like *absolutely, luminous,* and *indissolubly* with unfailing success.

It does not, however, sound inconsistent to use *yoo* in the *duke* group and not use it in the *Luke* group. Many good speakers follow this pattern. In other words, it is no more inconsistent to say *dyook* but not *Lyook* than it is to say *kyoob* (*cube*) and not *Lyook*.

It is the too zealous attempt to adopt the *Lyook* and *syoot* pattern that causes people to say *rez-yoo-rec-tion* for *rezzerection* (*resurrection*), as mentioned above. They think the u should be long u instead of an obscure vowel.

Don't be persuaded that you must use a trilled r (even the " one-flap " r) in *spirit* and *spiritual*. Most English people use it in these words naturally; but they also use it naturally in every word containing an r sound between two vowel sounds, as *very, American, material, arrow, awry,* etc. The trilled r is not natural to Americans. Formerly it was always employed in stage diction, especially Shakespearean delivery. But even in these fields the untrilled American r is becoming accepted, at least in America. Certainly a trilled r has no place in the speech of an American lay speaker. It belongs with broad a's. However, regardless of whether or not it is appropriate or desirable, there is one practical consideration that should prevent any American from trying to use it: it is almost impossible to be consistent in its use. To use it in *spirit* and *spiritual* and *American* and to forget it in other words (in any other word) is like saying, " I cahn't find it and you cain't either." It is like wearing golf shoes with an evening dress.

What about *blessed, cursed, hallowed,* etc.? Webster gives two syllables for *blessed,* adding that it is " sometimes, as in verse, blĕst, but usually only when spelled blest." *Cursed* may have two syllables or only one (*kurst*). *Hallowed* is two syllables but is " in the solemn or liturgical style, often *hal-o-ed.*"

To explain the pronunciation of *Jesus* may seem surprising. Surely it would seem that that would be a word everyone would know how to pronounce. Yes, but sometimes people are too careful in pronouncing it, using a full short u (as in *up*) in the second syllable, instead of an obscure vowel (as in *caucus*). It should be not *Jezuss* but *Jeez̒ss.*

It is hard to please everyone with the pronunciation of *God.* It should not be *Gahd,* with a completely unrounded a sound, as in *yacht.* Nor should it be *Gawd,* with a closely rounded a sound, as in *caught.* It should be just between *Gahd* and *Gawd.*

To the surprise of many people who look it up for the first time, *artificer* is accented on the second syllable instead of on the first. (The accent is on *tiff* rather than on *art.*)

Notice that *genealogy* ends in *-alogy,* not *-ology.* The third syllable rhymes with *Sal,* not with *Sol.* The first e may be either short or long.

The first syllable of *banquet* is not *ban-* but *bang-.*

Don't struggle to sound the i in *marriage* and *carriage.* They have only two syllables and rhyme with *disparage.*

Influence is accented on the first syllable.

The *arch-* in *archangel* is pronounced like *arc.* Elsewhere that prefix is rhymed with *parch.*

The accent falls on the first syllable of *vehement.*

The s in *visage* sounds like a z.

Webster's now allows the first o in *bosom* to have the sound of oo in *foot* or of oo in *food.*

Long a as in *ale* is used in *amen* but broad a as in father may be used and, in singing, must be used.

The suffixes, *-ness, -ed, -es,* etc., have already been discussed, in Part 1 of this chapter. The suffix *-ment* falls somewhat into this category. Almost no American says *judg-meant,* with a full short e in the second syllable, in conversation. The e in *judgment* should be an obscure vowel, as in *silent*—when *silent* is pronounced naturally and spontaneously. As Webster's points out, the large majority of words with this obscure vowel e marking are pronounced with the obscure vowel sound, not with short e as in *end.* Short e should not be used in these words except, perhaps, when you are being extremely emphatic or when you are singing. It is *judgm'nt, commandm'nt, diffid'nt, Jerusal'm*—but not *Jerusalumm,* of course. And don't feel that you need the short e sound to make the word clearly audible. No matter how large the auditorium in which you are reading, you don't need anything but the obscure vowel here. If you had to say " above the sofa " in Convention Hall, you would still pronounce both a's as obscure vowels. You wouldn't use short a's or long a's in order to be understood. You don't need to change your pronunciation to achieve audibility; change your articulation.

Israel and *Isaiah* are words that give speakers much needless distress. Don't think you have to struggle to say *Izz-ray-ell.* If you naturally say it, all right. But if your usual pronunciation of it is *Izz-ri-'l* (both i's short, as in *ill*) don't bother to change. Webster's gives both, and unless you are a radiant exception you probably have a few things to do to your diction that are more important than changing from one accepted pronunciation to another. People usually have a feeling that the pronunciation they don't use is better than the one they use. Before you change from one pronunciation to another, be sure of two things: (1) that the one you use is not approved; (2) that the one you adopt is authoritative. It is better to be plain and right than fancy and wrong.

If you naturally say *Eye-zay-uh,* don't feel that you must learn to say *Eye-zi-uh,* with a long i in the second syllable, to rhyme with *by.* Webster's allows both. Many people become concerned when they notice that Webster puts a y in the marking of *Eye-zay-uh* (ī-zā′-yá). Don't let this bother you. The long a in the second syllable is a "smiling" vowel and when you go from a smiling vowel to an obscure vowel you automatically make something of a y sound. You would have to work hard not to.

Words ending in *-ary, -ery,* and *-ory* have an American pronunciation and a British pronunciation. *Temporary,* as an example, is pronounced by most Americans with the heavy accent on the first syllable and a light accent on the third. The a in the third syllable is pronounced as a short e, rhyming with *very.* The British, however, not only do not give a light accent to the third but even clip it to an obscure vowel, sometimes leaving it out altogether: *tempor'y.* Don't feel, if it is not natural to you, that you must begin to say *diction'ry, observat'ry, cemet'ry.* The effect of such an attempt can often be deplorable. Worse than that, it can be funny. There is the Texas woman who decided she wanted to sound British and began to clip words like these. Unfortunately she still had, among other Southwestern speech patterns, the one that causes Southerners and Southwesterners to say *tin cints* for *ten cents, twinty min* for *twenty men,* etc. So, when she tried to call a cemetery a *cemet'ry,* she called it a symmetry.

An Eastern woman, trying to adopt this pronunciation, became so confused that she accidentally called *Il Trovatore* " Il Trovat'ry."

Most audiences find good, honest mistakes less annoying—and less funny—than affectations.

A plea will now be entered for one of the most mistreated words in the English language: *effect.* Speakers in public, speakers in private, and speakers over the radio do violence to this word. It is mispronounced when sung, spoken, or whispered. The word is not *ee-fect.* The first e may be short e (as in *end*), short i (as in *ill*), or an obscure vowel (just a rapid, unstressed *uh*), but it may not be long e. Never long e. To pronounce it long in this word violates a law or at least a rule of English spelling: a double consonant always shortens (or obscures) the preceding vowel. You can't divide the word into any form that would provide for pronouncing it *ee-fect.* It can't be divided *e-ffect,* as that would make the second syllable start with a double consonant. If you divide it *ef-fect,* the consonant shortens the e. If you divide it *eff-ect,* which would be possible phonetically though not etymologically, the double consonant shortens the e.

One reason that people pronounce it *ee-fect* is that they are trying to distinguish between *effect* and *affect*. They will say, " I mean *ee-fect* not *a-fect* " (with long a), when they should make the distinction by saying, " I mean *ef-fect* " (with short e) " not *af-fect* " (with short a).

The same mistake is made in words like *oppress* and *offense*. The double consonants shorten or obscure the preceding o in each case. Usually each starts with an obscure vowel, but if you want to contrast *oppress* with *impress*, for instance, you sound the o short, not long.

Knowledge of this rule would prevent anyone from making the mistake mentioned in the pronunciation of *resurrection*. The double r would either shorten or obscure the u. (It obscures the u.)

Do not scorn to use obscure vowels. They are one mark of an experienced speaker. The student or the inexperiencd speaker or reader often strives to pro-nounce ev-e-ry let-ter in al-most a clock-work-man style. The professional speaker, on the other hand, has become so much accustomed to using good diction that he is easy, comfortable, and casual, just as a person who has always had good manners is less stiff than someone who is afraid he will do the wrong thing. The experienced speaker is more likely than the beginner to use obscure vowels in the first syllables of words like *affection, obscure, connect, approach,* etc.

The purpose of these two sections is twofold. It is to help you pronounce the words discussed and, still more, to help you use and understand the dictionary. That is why the elementary device of using rhymes to explain the pronunciations has been used instead of writing them out fully in diacritical markings. When you are sure that you understand the pronunciations of these words, as illustrated by rhymes, go to the dictionary and see how they are marked. Then this will help you in looking up other words.

No attempt has been made to help you to overcome local speech patterns. Most people have some, but these patterns are not within the province of this book.

Remember that the English language is fluid. Every day the pronunciations and usages in English are changing. Accepted usages become obsolescent and then obsolete. Scorned pronunciations gain approval. It is safer to say that a certain pronunciation is "accepted" or "not accepted" than to say it is "correct" or "incorrect." Both time and geography enter into the question. What is "correct" today may be "incorrect" tomorrow, and vice versa. What is "correct" here is "incorrect" there, and vice versa.

A dictionary does not set out to say: "You must use this pronunciation. That one you must not use." When a dictionary lists a pronunciation of a word, it is supposed to mean that at the present time that is the way the majority of educated speakers and readers pronounce the word.

EXERCISES

1. "Who hath ears to hear, let him hear" (Matthew 13:9).

2. "And there went out a fame of him through all the region round about" (Luke 4:14).

3. "And there was delivered unto him the book of the prophet Esaias" (Luke 4:17).

4. "And the Lord God planted a garden eastward in Eden; and there he put the man whom he had formed" (Genesis 2:8).

5. "Now if ye be ready that at what time ye hear the sound of the cornet, flute, harp, sackbut, psaltery, and dulcimer, and all kinds of musick, ye fall down and worship the image which I have made; well . . ." (Daniel 3:15).

6. "And she being with child cried, travailing in birth, and pained to be delivered" (Revelation 12:2).

7. "Then Joseph her husband, being a just man, and not willing to make her a publick example, was minded to put her away privily" (Matthew 1:19).

8. "Looking for and hasting unto the coming of the day of God, wherein the heavens being on fire shall be dissolved . . ." (II Peter 3:12).

9. "I being in the way, the Lord led me to the house of my master's brethren" (Genesis 24:27).

10. "Let this mind be in you, which was also in Christ Jesus: Who, being in the form of God, thought it not robbery to be equal with God" (Philippians 2:5, 6).

11. "This is now the third time that Jesus showed himself to his disciples, after that he was risen from the dead" (John 21:14).

12. "And the Lord said unto Abram, after that Lot was separated from him, Lift up now thine eyes" (Genesis 13:14).

13. "And the ruler of the synagogue answered with indignation because that Jesus had healed on the sabbath day" (Luke 13:14).

14. "And it came to pass the third day after that I was delivered, that this woman was delivered also" (I Kings 3:18).

15. "Until the day in which he was taken up, after that he through the Holy Ghost had given commandments unto the apostles . . ." (Acts 1:2).

Answer Book

1. Read this as though *He,* the understood antecedent of *Who,* were expressed: He who hath ears to hear, let him hear. You will find that you subdue *Who* and read *Who* on a rather low pitch. Read it in the same way when you leave out *He.* (Relative and Interrogative *Who.*)

2. *There* is expletive, subdued. (Adverb *There* and Expletive *There,* etc.)

3. *There* is expletive, subdued. (Adverb and Expletive *There.*)

4. *There* is an adverb, not subdued. (Adverb and Expletive *There.*)

5. *That* should be subdued. (Special Constructions.)

6. This is a simple participial construction, not an absolute. In order to save the pronoun *she* for its proper predicate, *cried,* you pause before the participle, *being,* which merely modifies *she* instead of being the predicate of *she.* (Participial Constructions.)

7. *Being* is a participle modifying *Joseph her husband.* It is not

an absolute construction. In order to keep *Joseph her husband* for its real verb, *was*, you pause before *being*. (Refrain: you do not pause because there is a comma there. You pause because the sense requires a pause. The pause and the comma are both effects of the sense.) (Participial Constructions.)

8. If you do not pause before *being*, perhaps pausing before *the heavens* and after *fire*, you leave nothing for *shall be dissolved*. This is not an absolute construction. *Being* is simply a participle modifying *heavens* and there should be a slight pause between *heavens* and *being*. (Participial Constructions.)

9. *I being in the way* is an absolute construction. *I* is subject of *being;* so you make no pause between *I* and *being*. If you should pause between them, it would imply that you were going to read something like this: I, being in the way, was led by the Lord. (Participial Constructions.)

10. Here you have a poser. *Who*, at the beginning of verse 6, is the subject of *thought*. *Being* is a simple participle modifying *Who*. It does not form an absolute construction. It would be easy enough just to pause after *Who* but in order to do so you have to give some emphasis to *Who* and it happens that *Who* is " a connecting word followed by a parenthetical expression set off by commas." As we saw in Chapter V, the conversationally natural way to read such a construction is not to stress the relative word and not to pause after it. So how shall we read this verse? We have a choice between clearness of meaning and naturalness of style. Clearness seems even more important than naturalness and so we probably should pause after *Who*. A construction like this would almost never arise in everyday speech, which is usually informal and simple in structure. That is why our conversational way of speaking is always both clear and natural. (Participial Constructions.)

11. Subdue second *that*. (Miscellaneous Special Constructions.)

12. Subdue *that*. (Miscellaneous Special Constructions.)

13. Subdue *that*. (Miscellaneous Special Constructions.)
14. Subdue first *that*. (Miscellaneous Special Constructions.)
15. Subdue *that*. (Miscellaneous Special Constructions.)

VII

STILL MORE ABOUT EMPHASIS

Do We Ever Stress an Old Idea?

BEWARE OF APPLYING the principle of subduing old words or even old ideas with slavish invariability. You will find numerous places where you will feel that you will need to deviate from this natural and logical pattern, and you must be alert to them. Often a word that seems to present an old idea may on more mature examination prove to carry a new thought or at least an implied contrast. Sometimes, though very rarely, we may even stress deliberately what actually is an old idea.

Below are a few of the conditions under which we may seem to deviate from the pattern of subduing old ideas. These are not violations of the principle; they are merely applications of it in an extended and more advanced way. They are not rules that I have made up or exceptions I "allow." They are not patterns that you or I may think "sound good." There is a valid reason for each one. Furthermore, they are the stress patterns we would use in unrehearsed conversation, because we would then be thinking about the meaning alone and not about how to bring out the meaning, which is the problem the oral reader must face. When we are just talking, the meaning brings itself out.

These instances by no means exhaust the list: there are other conditions under which we spontaneously and reasonably stres old ideas—or what seem at first glance to be old ideas. I shal probably think of more before these sentences reach print, anc so may you, but these following cases should help you to be alert to see possibilities. Also, they should encourage you to go ahead and stress a word that your common sense and your ear tell you should be stressed, even though it seems to contradict the subduing principle, or any other principle or pattern. *Never try to fit the sentence to the principle; fit the principle to the sentence.*

(1) *Newness due to distance from original word.* When the idea, or even the exact word, has been said so long before that the hearer has probably stopped thinking about it, you must re-stress it, as it becomes new again. *An old idea does not stay old forever.*

You have a string of old ideas at the end of John 14:25 and 26. "These things have I spoken unto you, being yet present with you. But the Comforter, which is the Holy Ghost, whom the Father will send in my name, he shall teach you all things, and bring all things to your remembrance, whatsoever I have said unto you." *I* and *said* and *you* are all old. Can you emphasize any of them? Can one of them be construed as contrasted with anything? You can hardly work up a case for *said*, as *spoken, teach,* and *bring to remembrance* are all related to saying something. Many people just land comfortably on the final *you*, but doesn't this stress imply a contrast? With what? Well, it would have to be a contrast with somebody else. Is there an implication of having said something to someone else? If not, what about stressing *I*? You said *I* in the preceding verse, but isn't this last *I*, like the first *I*, in heavy contrast with two intervening words, *Comforter* and *he*? So we would stress *I* and subdue *said* and *you*.

By the time you have said *oppressions* and *oppressed,* in Ecclesiastes 4:1, *oppressors* would seem very old and not worthy of emphasis. "So I returned, and considered all the oppressions that are done under the sun: and behold the tears of such as were oppressed, and they had no comforter; and on the side of their oppressors there was power; but they had no comforter." *Oppressions* would have light new-idea emphasis and *oppressed* would be subdued, *tears* receiving light stress merely as a new idea. But before you get around to saying *oppressors*, its opposite (*comforter*) has been said; so *oppressors* is stressed because of its contrast to *comforter*.

(2) *Newness due to intervening opposite.* Even if you have

quite recently said the word, if its opposite has been said in the meanwhile, you re-stress the repeated word. It has become new again.

If you say, "She wore a black hat and they wore white hats," *white* will be stressed as a contrast with *black*: but, if you say, "She wore a black hat and they wore white hats and I'll wear a black hat," you will stress *black* again, even though it is an old idea, because in the meantime has come its opposite, *white*. This makes the second *black* new again, in contrast to *white*.

This instance is so obvious that you would stress it this way automatically, but in some cases you have to do a bit of delving. In John 14:25-26, *he* is old, meaning the same thing as *Comforter*, but a closer look shows that both *he* and *Comforter* are contrasted with a word farther back: *I*. The meaning is brought out better by stressing *he*, thus showing its contrast with *I*, than by subduing it because it is the same as *Comforter*. Naturally, *Comforter* would need a contrast stress, as opposed to *I*.

We must not make rigid rules of these principles and patterns. The sentences you read are subject to coloration from surrounding sentences and you must weigh the relative importance of the possible contrasts and resemblances of ideas. One reader will consider one point to be of primary importance; another will select the other point. In this way they will both bring out logical meaning but will not sound alike.

This does not mean that we can read just any old way. Although many sentences afford a choice of phrasing and emphasis, there are many phrases and whole sentences which need to be read one way by everyone and in any context. It would be difficult to find a setting in which the reading of II Kings 6:16 could change. (See Exercise 50, page 52.)

(3) *Newness due to contrast-versus-similarity.* When it is more important to contrast a word with something further back than to show its similarity to a closer word, we stress an old idea. The illustration from John given three paragraphs back might come under this heading.

Matthew 14:29 reads, "And he said, Come. And when Peter was come down out of the ship, he walked on the water, to go to Jesus." The second *he* is certainly old, referring to *Peter,* in the preceding line. Subduing it would make sense, but see how the verse springs to life when you stress this *he,* contrasting it with *Jesus,* who was walking on the water back in verse 25.

Sometimes the word with which the contrast is made is not even expressed. In I Corinthians 2:13 ("Which things also we speak, not in the words which man's wisdom teacheth, but which the Holy Ghost teacheth; comparing spiritual things with spiritual.") the obvious way is to subdue the second *spiritual.* This leads to stressing *with,* as the only new idea available. This makes sense, but does it make the point? Wouldn't it strengthen the reading to stress the second *spiritual,* thus implying a contrast with an (implied) *material?* That is, comparing spiritual things with spiritual rather than with material?

Occasionally the use of this point of your technique will turn up a gem of meaning that you may never have seen. "The prophet that hath a dream, let him tell a dream; and he that hath my word, let him speak my word faithfully." (Jeremiah 23:28.) A cursory application of the new and old principle would probably lead you to stress the first *dream,* the first *tell,* the first *word,* and possibly *speak*; to subdue the first *him,* the second *dream,* the second *him,* the second *word,* and possibly *speak*; and to stress *faithfully* without a pause before it. This would make *faithfully* the main point of the verse.

But take another look. Work from the latter part of the sentence and forget about *faithfully* for a minute. Consider the rest of the sentence. True, the second *word* is a repetition; but isn't it in contrast with something? How about contrasting it with the second *dream?* Try a very heavy contrast by stressing the second *dream,* too.

Now is *speak* really a new idea? Isn't it the same as *tell?* So how about subduing *speak?* All right, let's re-consider the second *him.* Yes, it's old, but isn't it in contrast with the first *him?* So experiment with stressing them both. Now what have we? "The prophet that hath a *dream,* let *him* tell a *dream*; and he that hath my *word,* let *him* speak my *word* . . ." Then we go back and pick up *faithfully.* We stress it (it's new) but is it the main point of the verse now? Even though we emphasize it, a pause in front of it gives its proper value in proportion to the whole sentence.

With this type of emphasis you can work out a most enlightening reading of II Corinthians 11:3. "But I fear, lest by any means, as the serpent beguiled Eve through his subtilty, so your minds should be corrupted from the simplicity that is in Christ." If you have just read the serpent scene in the third chapter of Genesis, the carry-over is thrilling. But, even if you read it alone, it has a sort of built-in carry-over, since the analogy automatically takes your thought back to Genesis. So, although almost all the words carry new ideas, you will find that you subdue most of them. Bearing in mind the episode in Genesis, you would say that *serpent, beguiled, Eve, subtilty,* and *corrupted* are certainly old. *Minds* is implied old, since mentioning Eve implies Eve's mind. Therefore, you would subdue *minds,* leaving only *your* as new. *Your* is not only new; it is a contrast. With what? With *Eve.* Isn't there a contrast implied between Eve's mind and your minds?

Here is another example of not subduing an old idea (*Eve*) because it is more important to contrast it with something.

(4) *Newness of definition of a repeated word.* Often the same word, when repeated, may have a very different meaning from the first use of it. In I Peter 5:7, readers often subdue *careth* because they have just read *care.* ("Casting all your care upon him; for he careth for you.") Sometimes, because they feel they have to have something to emphasize, they stress *you* or *he* or both, even though these are indisputably old ideas, echoing *your* and *him.* *Careth,* however, is an entirely different idea from *care,* because *care* means *burden* and *careth* means *looks after.* Therefore, you would consider *careth* a new idea, and you would stress it, subduing *you.*

"Who hath saved us, and called us with an holy calling . . ." (II Timothy 1:9) Many readers subdue *calling,* having just said *called,* but doesn't *called* mean *summoned,* and *calling* mean *vocation?* If you said ". . . he hath summoned you with a holy vocation," wouldn't you then stress both *holy* and *vocation* as new ideas?

(5) *Newness of mood.* Sometimes the identical word repeated,

or a different form of the identical word, may have exactly the same meaning, or definition, and yet have a distinctly different flavor. (I apologize for the high-toned word here; actually, I can avoid using it by saying that sometimes the newness is newness of mood, or change of mood, as from the subjunctive mood to the indicative.) Exodus 4 has an instance of this. In verse three ("And he said, Cast it on the ground. And he cast it on the ground . . .") I had always emphasized both *cast*s and the first *ground*, subduing the second *ground*. Then one day it suddenly occurred to me that perhaps I should subdue the second *cast*, as an old idea, as well as an old word. When I tried that, the second *ground* flew up and hit me, as I had to have something to stress. When I had removed the stress from the second *cast*, it automatically lighted on the second *ground*, which, I realized, was just as old as *cast*. All the other words canceled out as old ideas; so, even though I seemed to be departing from the principle of subduing the old idea, I followed common sense (the best principle of all!) and went on stressing the second *cast* and subduing the second *ground*. Later I realized the logical reason for this emphasis: I saw that I had actually been following the principle of subduing but with more advanced and thoughtful application. Actually, the second *cast*, although an old word with an old meaning, has a decidedly different flavor (there's that word again!) from that of the first *cast*. The first is mere potentiality, a command, in the imperative mood. (Maybe he will cast it; maybe he won't.) But the second *cast* denotes actuality; it shows a change of mood, being confirmatory, in the indicative mood. (He *did* cast it on the ground.) In modern English we would use the auxiliary verb *did*, which shows confirmation or actuality. Lacking it in the Bible translation, we have to let the second *cast* carry the whole load.

This word pattern is like the television commercial advertising a certain breakfast food. The slogan is "So-and-So gives you get-up-and-go." A listener was said to have written in "I fed my husband So-and-So and it gave him so much get-up-and-go that he *got* up and *went!*" She could have said, ". . . that he *did* get up and *did* go." But she omitted the auxiliaries and placed the emphasis on the old words with a new flavor.

(6) *Newness of tense.* "Father, glorify thy name. Then came there a voice from heaven, saying, I have both glorified it, and will glorify it again." (John 12:28.) *Glorified* is old. The only newness here shows up in the change of tense from *glorify* to *have glorified.* *Have* brings out the contrast and is emphasized. In fact, even if you left out *glorified* and ended with *have* it would make complete sense. *Both* is another dispensable idea and can be subdued. The last *glorify* is old; again, the newness comes in the change of tense, from present perfect (*have glorified*) to future. Since *will* indicates the futurity (the contrast), *will* is stressed. Again, omitting *glorify* and *it,* old ideas, would not deplete the sentence. (Of course I don't recommend actually leaving them out! We're just experimenting with the new and old ideas, the indispensable and dispensable.) Remember: *any word you can leave out without changing the meaning you need not and should not stress.*

Art and *wast* contrast the present and the future tense in Revelation 11:17. *Art to come* is future, with *to come* expressing the futurity. We stress *art, wast,* and *come.* "Saying, We give thee thanks, O Lord God Almighty, which art, and wast, and art to come . . ."

This last example almost anyone would emphasize as indicated without having to stop to reason it out. The sixth and seventh headings are given only to add to the list of circumstances under which we do stress old ideas, often without noticing.

(7) *Newness of voice.* "For now we see through a glass, darkly; but then face to face: now I know in part; but then shall I know even as also I am known." (I Corinthians 13:12.) Almost without giving it a thought we stress *known,* but the technique behind it is that, although the idea behind *known* is the same as that behind *know,* and although the meaning of *known* is old, there is something new about it. The newness lies in the voice, in the switch from active voice to passive.

(8) *No newness at all: complete restatement.* Sometimes, as in Psalms and Proverbs, the second half of a verse or sentence may be an exact restatement of the first. Each word in the second half may be a precise synonym of one in the first. What do you

do? Well, obviously, you can't subdue a whole clause; you can't mutter an entire half of a long verse into your beard. Examine the words closely to see whether one word (idea) might possibly be considered as a bit newer than the others; if so, you can stress that one. But sometimes you will find that the ideas in all the words are equally old. In this case, don't worry about it. Just read the second half, with the old ideas, as if it were the first thing you were reading and stress the second half as you would if you hadn't read the first half at all.

In Proverbs 2:3 (". . . if thou criest after knowledge, and liftest up thy voice for understanding") *liftest up thy voice for* is the same as *criest after*; *thy* and *thou* refer to the same thing (the same idea); *knowledge* and *understanding* also are similar, but, since there is perhaps some very fine distinction between them, you might logically stress *understanding*. Others might consider the whole thing an idea-by-idea repetition of the first half, as in Proverbs 4:14, where the entire second half is undoubtedly a precise restatement of the first. ("Enter not into the path of the wicked, and go not in the way of evil men.") *Go in* is substantially the same as *enter into*, *not* identical with *not*, *the way* the same as *the path*, and *of evil men* the same as *the wicked*. You cannot just mumble the whole second clause; so you must cast about for some word or words to lean on. Well, how would you say "go not in the way of evil men" if it opened the sentence? Probably you would stress *evil*. If so, stress it when you read the entire verse.

(9) *Newness of relationship*. Occasionally you will find a clause in which all the ideas have been presented but in which two of the repeated words, retaining their very same meanings, may have new positions in relation to each other, as in Genesis 32:29. ("And Jacob asked him, and said, Tell me, I pray thee, thy name. . . .") Assuming that you have first read verses 24 through 28, *Jacob* is old, and so are *asked* and *him*, since *him* refers to the one that Jacob was wrestling with. But it would sound forced and meaningless to subdue everything; so what can you do? Well, although *Jacob* and *him* are not new, their relationship to each other, their relative positions, are new. The man

had already asked Jacob a question, in verse 27: "And he said unto him, What is thy name? And he said, Jacob." In verse 29, Jacob asked the man. *Asking* is old, but the asker and the asked have changed places. The asker has become the asked, and the asked the asker. So you stress *Jacob* and *him.* You stress it as you would a sentence like "I helped him and *he* helped *me,*" or "*I* helped *him* and *he* helped *me.*"

The heavy double contrast is so apparent in Matthew 3:14 that we naturally stress *I, thee, thou,* and *me.* ("But John forbad him, saying, I have need to be baptized of thee, and comest thou to me?") Although *thou* and *me* are old, same as *thee* and *I,* it is their relationship that is new.

10)   *Newness of aspect; appositives and synonyms.* Some readers try to subdue any word which is a synonym of some word just read. Applying too inflexibly the principle of subduing old ideas, they reason that any synonym, being naturally an old idea, should be subdued. If you read, "The Governor is his father," even though *father* and *Governor* are not only synonyms but also actually one and the same person, it would not make sense to say "The *Governor* is his father," emphasizing *Governor* and toning down *father,* as that would imply that someone had just said that someone else was his father. (Never fail to examine your implication.) Even though *Governor* and *father* are identical, you emphasize *father* because it is a different aspect of the same man. The paternal aspect is a new idea, distinguished from the gubernatorial aspect.

An appositive (a word which specifically defines or identifies another) is by its very nature an old idea, but, as in the preceding case, is a new phase of the idea, and is therefore stressed in conversation. If you say, "The Governor, his father, is very popular" you will naturally stress *Governor* and also *father,* which is the appositive, the word in apposition with *Governor,* the word that identifies *Governor.* If you subdue *father,* you would imply that he has more than one father. (The *Governor,* his father, in contradistinction to his other father or fathers.)

If you speak of "George Washington, a great general, our country's first President," you will agree that *general* and *President* are synonyms of *George Washington.* A synonym is defined as a word that means the same or almost the same as another word. So you might argue that, since *general* and *President* mean the same as *George Washington,* they are old ideas and should be subdued; but your common sense will keep you from arriving at any such conclusion. You don't need to subdue any synonym simply because it is a synonym, since a synonym presents some new facet of the original word, a new aspect. Otherwise the two words would not be needed in the language. Therefore, you would give a light new-idea emphasis to *general* and also to *President.* I think this would apply to the reading of any synonyms.

(11) *Newness in the thought of the speaker.* Sometimes, especially in the reading of direct conversation, we have to ask ourselves not what is the new idea in the sentence but what is new in the thought of the speaker, or even what does the speaker think is new in the thought of the hearer.

In reading Isaiah 29:11-12 people sometimes think part of the way through the relationship of ideas and fail to go the final step.

"And the vision of all is become unto you as the words of a book that is sealed, which men deliver to one that is learned, saying, Read this, I pray thee: and he saith, I cannot; for it is sealed: And the book is delivered to him that is not learned, saying, Read this, I pray thee: and he saith, I am not learned." At first glance you might heavily stress *he,* the second *I,* and *learned,* in verse 12. But remember that *I am not learned* is direct conversation. "He" doesn't know that you have just read to them about how somebody else said that he couldn't read the book; so he wouldn't say *"I am not learned,"* since he isn't thinking of himself in comparison with anyone else. He would simply use a light new-idea emphasis on *learned.* However, you could emphasize *he* in verse 12, because this is part of the narrative. *You* are speaking (reading) now, and you do know that you have just read them about how the first one said he couldn't read it.

If this verse were in indirect discourse, you could stress it like this: And the book is delivered to one that is not learned saying to read it: and *he* says that *he* is not *learned.* In this wording *you* are saying the whole thing, and you do know that the other one has said he couldn't read it because it was sealed.

If Mark 14:12 had been written in indirect discourse, you

would subdue the second *passover*: And the first day of unleavened bread, when they killed the passover, his disciples asked him where he wanted them to go and prepare for him to eat the passover. You would give a very light new-idea emphasis to *eat.* However, as it is really written, you couldn't do this, because his disciples, who were the ones doing the talking, didn't know of your reading about killing the passover. "And the first day of unleavened bread, when they killed the passover, his disciples said unto him, Where wilt thou that we go and prepare that thou mayest eat the passover?" Accordingly, wouldn't you simply give a light stress to the second *passover*? Isn't it new in *their* thought?

Always watch this when you are reading a mixture of direct talking and narrative. However, do not carry it past a certain point. If you uncompromisingly stick with the policy of stressing and subduing according to what is in the thought of the one actually speaking, you may fail to make the point of some well-planned carry-over. Sometimes you may decide it is justifiable to fudge a bit and read the dialogue with the stress you would use if it were presented as indirect discourse.

(12) *Reiteration.* Sometimes we stress an old word which signifies an entirely old idea, merely to reiterate it. We keep pounding away at it, to hammer it in. Suppose you have written in a speech, "We must preserve our national integrity. That's the only way we can prosper. That's the only way we can remain sound. That's the only way we can maintain the world's respect." At first glance it might seem logical to stress the new ideas, *remain sound* and *maintain the world's respect,* and to subdue *That's the only way* the second and third times it is said. But this is where rigid application of technique should yield to art, which is more flexible. It may well be more effective to keep driving home the same point by re-stressing *That's the only way* each time and placing a lighter or an equal stress on the newer ideas.

Isaiah 33:22 reads: "For the Lord is our judge, the Lord is our lawgiver, the Lord is our king . . ." If this is your opening verse, you would probably emphasize the first *Lord,* and *judge, lawgiver,* and *king,* subduing the second and third *Lords* and all three *ours*. If, however, you have just been reading about false judges or other judges or kings, you may change your emphasis because of carry-over. You may stress the first *Lord* as before, only more heavily, but subdue *judge* as old, heavily stressing *our*, in implied contrast with whatever judge, lawgiver, or king you have just been reading about. You might then softpedal everything except *lawgiver* and *king*, as they could be considered to be distinguished from *judge*. However, this reading would take the juice out of the carry–over. A more effective way would be to keep pounding away at the contrast by subduing the new words, *lawgiver* and *king*, and re-stressing the second and third *Lords* and the second and third *ours*. "For the *Lord* is *our* judge, the *Lord* is *our* lawgiver, the *Lord* is *our* king. . . ." (Italics are mine.)

Please note that almost all these instances of stressing what seem like old ideas are not actually that. Although the words themselves are old, there is some sort of newness about them. There are only two conditions I have noticed up to this moment under which we stress a really old idea without any hint of newness. These are the times we do so (1) because we are deliberately pounding away at an old idea for reiteration (Heading 12) or (2) because the entire last half of a passage is completely old (Heading 8), in which case, not being able just to growl such a long thing, we have to proceed exactly as we would if we had not said anything beforehand.

I have devoted what may be an undue amount of space to discussing this relatively minor point, only to indicate under how many circumstances we automatically (in speaking) do emphasize what at first glance seems an old idea but is not.

Except for reiteration and restatement, we always reach for some kind of newness when we emphasize.

Do We Ever Subdue a New Idea?

Just as we often emphasize an old idea, so we often subdue a new idea, or what may look like a new idea. The first two verses of the third chapter of Genesis read: "Now the serpent was more subtil than any beast of the field which the Lord God had made. And he said unto the woman, Yea, hath God said, Ye shall not eat of every tree of the garden? And the woman said unto the serpent, We may eat of the fruit of the trees of the garden." Look at Eve's speech. Is *garden* new? No. You've said not only the idea but the very word in verse one. *Trees* is old and so is *eat*. This leaves *fruit* and *We,* both of them being words that have not been said in these verses.

So do you emphasize *fruit?* Well, if you do, you imply that the serpent had meant they might eat of the leaves or the bark. Most people agree that the serpent implied fruit when he spoke of eating of the trees. This would make *fruit* implied old and we would subdue it.

Usually at this point people say, "There's no new word except *We.*" But is *We* new? When Eve says *We,* doesn't that mean the same thing that the serpent meant by *Ye?* Then *We* is old. At this juncture many people say, "There just isn't any new idea!" But there is. What about the little word *may?* Isn't it in contrast with an implied "may not" in verse one?

Try reading Eve's speech in this verse stressing *may* and subduing all the other words. You could even end the sentence with *may.* "We may." Remember: *any word you can leave out without changing the meaning you need not and should not stress.*

Just as we can stress old ideas in Isaiah 33:22 for the purpose of reiteration, so we can subdue two new ideas: *lawgiver* and *king.* (See page 186, Line 34.)

IMPORTANCE OF SUBDUING

We have said a great deal about stressing. What about subduing? Well, you simply can't have emphasis without subduing. How can you have a hill without a valley? How can you emphasize a word without de-emphasizing another? How can you have a highlight without a shadow?

Beware of emphasizing too many words. Some readers think that the more words they stress the more meaning they give out, the more convincing it sounds, but as a general thing stressing too many words steals the thunder from the one word, or the few words, that should be stressed in order to bring out the point.

Failure to subdue the old ideas, the meaningless or taken-for-granted words, is like failure to use enough shadows in your snapshot. Your picture is light-struck.

Shall I say it another way? Subduing the nonessential ideas is like clearing out the underbrush so that the big trees can grow. Otherwise, as the saying goes, you can't see the woods for the trees.

I have actually heard it said that to subdue any words in the Bible is irreverent. Well, stressing all the words rubs out the meaning and what could be more irreverent than omitting the meaning when reading the Bible? If you underscore a few words when writing a letter, you call special attention to those words, but if you underscore all the words you're right back where you started—with no emphasis at all.

I once listened to a Bible reader who pursued the soporific policy of stressing all words except the prepositions, conjunctions, and articles. All the rest of his sentences were like a plateau. It reminded me of the story of the man who found the pixies' hoard of gold. It was too heavy to carry home; so for the time being he hid it under a bush. He happened to have a yellow rag with him, which he tied on the bush so that he could find it the next day. The following morning he came back to the place, confidently expecting to find his gold and take it home. The pixies had tied a yellow rag on every bush in the clearing!

Most people can emphasize with the greatest of ease. It is sub-duing that presents the difficulty. Many will stress a word and then go right along and stress the following word, even though it should be subdued. This of course rubs out the emphasis from the preceding word. Don't hang your yellow rags on too many bushes!

More artistry is required for subduing than for stressing. Any soprano can yell but it requires a Zinka Milanov to produce a Milanov pianissimo. Almost any jalopy can function at a fair rate of speed, but smooth idling is a test of a fine car.

Sometimes a reader or actor forms a habit of pausing slightly after stressing a word, as if he were so overcome at having empha-sized that he has to take a little rest! This pause usually causes him to pounce on the next word with some stress, even though it may need to be subdued. Watch yourself on this point. If you find yourself pausing after a stressed word you will probably notice that you are emphasizing the next word, whether it should be emphasized or not. If the meaning does not require a pause after the stressed word and a loud-pedaling of the following word, practice going from the stressed word straight into the next one without pause.

Be chary with those yellow rags!

THE FUNCTIONS OF ITALICS

As a general thing, italicizing a word indicates that the idea it carries is important and that therefore the word should be emphasized. Italicizing of words in the King James Version of the Bible, however, does not necessarily signify the need of stress, because an italicized word there means simply that the word was supplied by the translators. Many of these italicized words are mere padding, inserted to smooth out the sentence. The latter part of Proverbs 27:10 reads: ". . . *for* better *is* a neighbor *that is* near than a brother far off." If you omit the italicized words, the meaning is still perfectly clear.

Sometimes, realizing this, people come to the comfortable conclusion that they can subdue every italicized word in the Bible. This policy would be convenient but it is too simple, as you can see from examining the italicized words as you read. Although usually they are not important, there are instances where they are the crucial words in the sentence and actually need emphasis. In Exodus 4:7, Moses is told to put his leprous hand into his bosom and then pluck it out. The verse concludes with the statement that ". . . it was turned again as his *other* flesh." You see that you could not omit *other* and still have the sentence make sense. Rather, you have to stress it, because *other* is a contrast with the flesh of his hand.

It is possible that, when italics is used on the important word, the idea-carrying word, it is employed not because the translator felt that the passage needed the word merely for polish but because the word may have been missing entirely from the original, because of a hole in the manuscript at that point or because of a smudge or stain or for some other reason.

In other books, however, the matter of italics presents several other aspects to be considered. Apparently most writers use italics for three main purposes:

(1) The first function is the usual one: to indicate importance and therefore emphasis. As in: One witness said that at two o'clock he saw the defendant going *up* the *back* stairs; another, that he saw her going *down* the *front* stairs.

(2) The second function is to set off a word which comes from a foreign language. As in: Their boredom persisted, although they tried many diversions to offset this *ennui*. And: The whole place glowed with an atmosphere of *gemütlichkeit*. And: He insisted upon a writ of *habeas corpus*.

Whether such words are to be emphasized depends entirely on the sense of the sentence. When they do require stress, it is occasioned by the meaning and not by the italicization. In the first illustrative sentence under this heading, you would probably not emphasize the italicized *"ennui,"* because it means substantially the same as "boredom," but you would stress it in this sentence: He enjoyed activities resulting from his many interests but his brother was burdened with persistent *ennui*. Here, *"ennui"* would be emphasized, not because it is italicized but because it is in heavy contrast to "activities" and "interests."

(3) A third function of italics is to show that some word is not serving what would seem to be its obvious role in the sentence. Read this aloud: The word list is blurred.

Didn't you emphasize *word*? Didn't you take it to mean that the list of words is blurred? Now read this: The word *list* is blurred.

This time you probably stressed *list,* and your reading indicated that a certain word was blurred and that the blurred word was *list*.

In the first version of the sample sentence, it looks as though *word* were used as an adjective to modify the noun *list,* but the italicization in the second version clearly shows that *word* is used as a noun and that *list* is not modified by *word* but that *list* is in apposition with *word*. In other words, here *list* means the same as *word;* it is not merely described by *word*. Therefore, although you slightly stress the italicized word, *list,* in the second sentence, you do it not because it is italicized but because the sense requires a slight stress. You do not give it anything like as much stress as you would in a setting like this: On my paper the word *best* is blurred but on her paper the word *list* is blurred. In this sentence there would be a heavy emphasis on *list,* to contrast it with *best.*

Other devices than italics, such as quotation marks, underlining, and heavy type, are sometimes used to perform this function of italics.

(Notice that in the paragraph beginning with "Didn't you emphasize *word?"* that *word* is italicized for the reason under discussion: for the third function of italics.)

One more point it would be well to clarify is the pronunciation of the word *italic* and related words. According to Webster's New International Dictionary, Second Edition, the Thorndike-Barnhart Comprehensive Desk Dictionary, and the Funk and Wagnalls Standard College Dictionary, the initial *i* is not long, as it is frequently heard, but short, so that the first two letters sound like the pronoun *it. Italic* comes from the noun *Italy* and means *Italian* (which also begins with a short *i*), or *deriving from Italy.*

CONCLUSION

All the ideas offered in this book are given in order to help you do just two things: first, to see and give out the real meaning; second, to sound natural. It might almost be summed up by saying that the new-and-old-idea principles attend to the first objective and that all the other headings are devoted to the second.

Make these principles your servants. Don't serve them. Don't try to shape the sentence to the principle you think should apply to it. Remember that at some time you will find an exception to almost every suggestion given in this book, not because the principles are not sound principles but because the context and the surrounding constructions sometimes affect the application of the principles. Always let common sense and good taste be your final test. Always remember that reading well is not just a science but an art supported by a scientific technique.